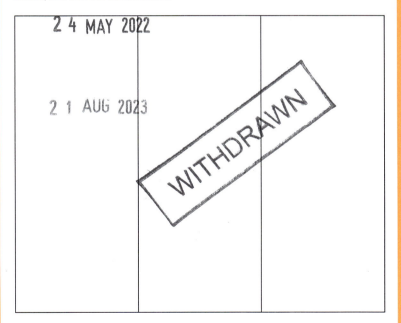

the right fat

First published in the United Kingdom in 2021 by
Pavilion
43 Great Ormond Street
London
WC1N 3HZ

ISBN 978-1-91166-321-8

A CIP catalogue record for this book is available from the British Library.
10 9 8 7 6 5 4 3 2 1

Reproduction by Rival Colour Ltd., UK
Printed and bound by L.E.G.O. S.p.A., Italy
www.pavilionbooks.com

Publisher: Helen Lewis
Photographer: Haarala Hamilton
Food stylist: Valerie Berry
Props stylist: Rachel Vere
Project editor: Sophie Allen
Design manager: Laura Russell
Design layout: Hannah Naughton
Illustrations: Nick Paul Jordan
Recipe analysis: Alina Tierney
Production manager: Phil Brown

the right fat

How to enjoy fats with
over 50 simple, nutritious
recipes for good health

Nicola Graimes

PAVILION

Speaking up for Fat

Dietary fat is essential to good health, yet for many it comes with negative connotations. Over the years we have been told fat is 'bad' and advised to switch to low-fat foods, including highly processed oils and hydrogenated margarines and spreads. But this dietary advice hasn't made us healthier and, if anything, has been detrimental to our well-being as obesity, heart disease and type 2 diabetes have exponentially increased. With so much misinformation and misunderstanding about fat, the time is right to stand up for this vital food group.

Not all fats are created equal. For many years saturated fat has been cast as the bad guy, linked with an increased risk of heart disease, but there is a growing body of evidence that questions this. If the saturated fat content is reduced to make a food low-fat, then what replaces it? The answer isn't good... In one study, replacing fat with sugar and refined carbs actually increased the risk of a heart attack. We are better off avoiding processed low-fat foods in favour of fresh, minimally processed foods that provide a wide range of nutrients and health benefits, even if they do contain fat. These are the right fats.

This book focuses on the positive attributes of the right fats from the right foods – an eclectic mix including extra virgin olive oil, nut and coconut oils, oily fish and other seafood, eggs, nuts, seeds, free-range poultry and, perhaps most controversially, meat and dairy, albeit from grass-fed, organically reared animals. It celebrates these ingredients, not only for their many health benefits, but also for the incredible diversity, taste and enjoyment they bring to our cooking and eating. Don't eat less fat or low fat, just eat the *right* fats.

Do We Really Need Fat?

We need fat to survive. Fat is a crucial source of energy, vital for cell growth, hormone regulation, blood clotting, brain and cognitive development (our brain is two-thirds fat). Fat helps the body absorb certain minerals and fat-soluble vitamins, including A, D, E and K, which need fat to be absorbed. Fat also supports good heart, gut, eye, skin, bone and mental health.

Fat plays an important role in making food satisfying to eat and helping us feel fuller for longer. Despite fat providing more calories per gram than protein or carbohydrates, people who eat a good range of healthy fats have been found to lose more weight than those who follow low-fat diets, or diets based on refined carbs and fat. However, good health is not about looking at one food group in isolation but how fat works in tandem with other macronutrients, such as good-quality protein and unrefined carbs, to support our physical and mental well-being.

Fat – the Basics

There are two types of fat: saturated and unsaturated; many foods are a combination of the two.

Saturated fatty acids (**SFAs**) include short-, medium- and long-chain fatty acids, all of which have different effects on health. Saturated fat is found mainly in animal products such as butter, whole milk, cream, cheese and meat as well as coconut oil and palm oil. It is solid at room temperature.

Unsaturated fat is made up of polyunsaturated and monounsaturated fat. It tends to be liquid at room temperature.

- **Monounsaturated fatty acids** (**MUFAs**) are found in olive oil, avocados and most nuts, including almonds, cashews, Brazils, pistachios and peanuts. Monounsaturated fat, or omega-9, is a good source of beneficial antioxidants and vitamins E and K. It comes with a long list of health attributes and numerous studies link MUFAs with a reduced risk of many chronic diseases, including cancer, heart disease, type 2 diabetes, Alzheimer's and arthritis.

- **Polyunsaturated fatty acids** (**PUFAs**) form two main types, omega-3 and omega-6, with some foods offering both. These essential fatty acids (EFAs) have to be provided by the diet as they cannot be made by the body. It is important to eat a balance of omega-3 and omega-6, with many of us eating too much of the latter and not enough of the former. Scientists have linked this imbalance to an increase in inflammatory conditions, including heart disease, diabetes and obesity.

Omega-3 comprises EPA (eicosapentaenoic acid), DHA (docosahexaenoic acid) and ALA (alpha-linolenic acid). EPA and DHA come mainly from animal foods such as oily fish, oysters, clams, mussels and meat and dairy from grass-fed cows (see page 30). ALA is supplied by plant-based foods, such as soya beans, seeds, seaweed and walnuts. From a nutritional perspective, the conversion of ALA in plant foods to EPA and DHA is not as effective as those from animal foods. Omega-3 comes with a list of impressive health benefits: it is vital for cell growth, brain function and development; improves heart health; and supports sleep, the gut, eyes, joints, bones, skin and mental health. It has been found to reduce age-related memory loss and fights inflammation in the body, which can contribute to many chronic diseases, such as type 2 diabetes, heart disease and certain cancers, including colon, prostate and breast as well as autoimmune diseases, such as Crohn's and arthritis.

Omega-6 is provided by plant-based oils, such as rapeseed, grapeseed and sunflower oil. Unfortunately, these tend to be highly processed fats, often linked to poor health and unstable when heated, so a better source is perhaps nuts and seeds. Omega-6 is an important source of energy in the body, however, omega-6 can also promote inflammation, whereas omega-3 can reduce it. Yes, inflammation can help fight infection and support immunity, but too much is the cause of many major chronic diseases. This explains why a balance of omega-6 and omega-3 is crucial – a ratio of 4:1 or less is recommended.

Right Fats – What are They?

Unsaturated and saturated fats are often labelled 'right' and 'wrong' or 'good' and 'bad' respectively, but many argue this is too simplistic and even misleading (see page 14).

Firstly, it doesn't take into account that many foods are a combination of both types of fat – we shouldn't dismiss outright foods high in saturated fat. A healthier way to look at 'right' versus 'wrong' fats is to consider how processed a food is and what else it contains in the way of additives, salt, sugar and other refined carbs. Increasingly, evidence suggests saturated fat from unprocessed foods (those as close to their original state as possible) may not be as harmful as suggested.

Many right-fat foods are at the heart of the much-praised Mediterranean diet (the traditional diet of countries bordering the Mediterranean Sea). Interestingly, people living around the Mediterranean are said to consume three times more fat than those on strict low-fat diets. A long-term Spanish study (PREDIMED) into the effects of the Mediterranean diet on those at high risk of cardiovascular disease showed impressive results for heart health. (Other research highlights possible protection against cancer and type 2 diabetes.) At the core of the Mediterranean diet is olive oil. This monounsaturated fat has been found to protect the heart, reducing the risk of cardiovascular disease by maintaining levels of HDL (good) cholesterol and reducing levels of LDL (bad) cholesterol (see page 13).

Nuts, seeds, fish and shellfish plus small amounts of meat and poultry are also mainstays of the Mediterranean diet (along with fruit and veg). These provide a range of good fats, particularly omega-3 fatty acids, which are as important in infancy as they are in old age. Bear in mind that omega-3 from seafood/animal sources, particularly oily fish, is more effective than that from plant sources, such as walnuts and flaxseeds/linseeds. That said, the latter are still a good choice, especially if you don't eat seafood.

Thumbs-up right fats:
- **Oils:** extra virgin olive oil, cold-pressed non-genetically modified (GM) rapeseed oil, sesame oil, walnut oil, hazelnut oil, hemp oil, avocado oil, coconut oil.
- **Meat and poultry:** grass-fed, preferably organic beef and lamb, free-range pork; organic chicken.
- **Fish and shellfish:** salmon, mackerel, sardines, sprats, herring, trout, pilchards, mussels, clams, oysters, crab, squid, sea bass, bream, turbot and halibut.
- **Eggs:** free-range, organic, preferably omega-3 enriched.
- **Dairy:** whole milk, cheese, cream, butter from grass-fed, preferably organically reared, cows, sheep and goats.
- **Nuts and seeds:** flaxseeds/linseeds, sesame, sunflower, hemp seeds, pumpkin seeds, walnuts, hazelnuts, Brazil, almonds, pecans, cashews.
- **Other:** soya beans, edamame, tofu, avocado.

Cholesterol

It's impossible to talk about fat without mentioning cholesterol. Cholesterol is crucial for the normal functioning of the body. It is a part of all cell membranes and is needed to make hormones, vitamin D and bile acids. Only a small amount comes from what we eat as about 80 per cent is made by the liver. Diet, exercise and genetic make-up all influence our cholesterol levels.

The relationship between saturated fat and cholesterol is more complicated than once believed. Saturated fat does increase levels of harmful low-density lipoproteins (LDL) cholesterol, which build up in the arteries, but it also increases beneficial high-density lipoproteins (HDL) cholesterol. HDL comes with a number of health benefits, particularly reducing the risk of heart disease.

What are 'Bad' Fats?

The impact of saturated fat on our health is a hot topic. Many believe that the focus on saturated fat as the bad guy is too much of a generalization and does not factor in the negative impact on health of industrially processed oils, trans fats, refined carbs, such as sugar and white flour, salt, additives and lack of exercise.

The demonization of fat, particularly saturated fat, began in the 1950s in the US. As heart disease increased in high-income countries, a study by scientist Ancel Keys pointed the finger at dietary fat and this research has continued to be influential. In some countries, including the US and UK, populations responded by eating more refined carbs and low-fat processed foods and this has reportedly led to a growth in heart disease, obesity and type 2 diabetes. There is a growing body of research that challenges these original studies, with some arguing that there is not enough reliable evidence that saturated fat increases the incidence of heart disease.

Highly processed, industrially refined, heat-treated and chemically deodorised fats are far more worthy of the 'bad' fat title. Widely grouped together as vegetable oils, these include trans fats (also known as partially hydrogenated oil or trans fatty acids). Trans fat is formed through an industrial process that adds hydrogen to vegetable oil, which extends its shelf life and makes it cheap to produce. Trans fats have no nutritional benefits and have been found guilty of clogging the arteries of people worldwide. They increase levels of harmful LDL cholesterol and reduce levels of beneficial HDL cholesterol – a double whammy when it comes to increasing the risk of heart disease. Trans fats also cause chronic inflammation in the body, which is the root cause of heart disease, type 2 diabetes, stroke and possibly cancer.

Trans fats have been banned in a number of countries, including the US, Denmark, Canada, Switzerland, Austria and Iceland, yet many continue to use them in processed foods (see list opposite). In the UK, the government introduced voluntary guidelines for food manufacturers in 2007 and while the use of trans fats significantly decreased, they are not yet banned. In 2018, the WHO (World Health Organization) launched the Replace initiative to eliminate industrially produced trans fats from food production by 2023 and the UK has agreed to fall in line.

The advice is to check food labels, yet you won't always find trans fats or partially hydrogenated fat listed. In the US, for instance, if a food contains less than 0.5g trans fats it can be labelled trans-fat-free, but if you eat more than the recommended serving amount, this can soon mount up. What is certain is that those countries that have banned trans fats have seen a fall in the number of deaths related to cardiovascular disease.

Look out for trans fats (partially hydrogenated oil) in:
- Mass-produced biscuits, cakes, cereal bars, crackers and baked goods
- Pastries, pies and sausage rolls
- Ready meals
- Fried fast foods, such as chips, burgers, fried fish and breaded chicken
- Chilled dough, bread and pizza
- Ready-made desserts
- Crisps, microwave popcorn and other snacks
- Peanut butter
- Spreads (butter substitutes and vegetable shortening)

Bear in mind, too, that some manufacturers simply list hydrogenated fat on the label without specifying whether a food is partially or fully hydrogenated. Fully hydrogenated fat, otherwise known as palm oil, does not contain trans fats but the scale and methods used in its production are having a devastating effect on the environment, wiping out native forest wildlife habitats and resulting in a vast increase in carbon emissions. Palm oil is cheap and used in many processed foods, often without us knowing. It has largely replaced trans fats in processed food, but that does not make it a good or healthy alternative.

Are Low-Fat Foods Healthy?

Processed low-fat foods are generally not a good option, even though the packaging may tell a different story. Unlike fruit and vegetables, which are naturally low in fat and brimming with nutrients, processed low-fat foods often contain other ingredients – namely sugar, high-fructose corn syrup and other refined carbs, salt, additives and fillers – to add bulk and flavour. Be wary of low-fat cereal bars, yogurts and drinks, low-fat sauces and dressings, reduced-fat peanut butter and spreads as more often than not they come with a list of undesirable extras.

How Much is 'Right'?

This book celebrates good fats, but this does not mean over-indulging on tubs of ice cream or bingeing on slabs of cheese. It means relishing the quality and variety of fats – in moderate amounts. Guidelines vary as to how much fat we should eat, so I have followed those recommended by the UK government. Although the figures differ for men and women, it is worth bearing in mind that they do not take into account age, genetic background or fitness. Nor do they factor in the quality or nutritional value of a fat.

Total fat:
- **High** – more than 17.5g fat per 100g
- **Low** – 3g or less per 100g or 1.5ml per 100ml for liquids
- **Fat free** – 0.5g or less per 100g or 100ml

Saturated fat:
- **High** – more than 5g saturates per 100g
- **Low** – 1.5g saturates or less per 100g; 0.75ml per 100ml for liquids
- **Fat free** – 0.1g saturates per 100g or 100ml

Total fat intake:
- 70g per day for women eating 2,000 calories
- 90g per day for men eating 2,500 calories
- Equates to 20–35 per cent of total recommended calories from fat

Saturated fat intake:
- **Men** – no more than 30g/1 oz saturated fat a day
- **Women** – no more than 20g/¾ oz saturated fat a day

The figure for saturated fat intake is quite generous when you consider a cup of whole milk contains around 4.5g saturated fat.

Shop & Cook the Right Fat Way

It's easy to undervalue the importance of fat in cooking. The role of fat is multifaceted: it can be the main ingredient; a cooking medium; and a form of seasoning – our food would certainly be a lot duller without it.

- Fats embellish flavour: a splash of sesame oil added to a stir-fry before serving becomes a seasoning; a knob of butter stirred into a risotto adds a layer of richness; a drizzle of walnut oil lifts a regular salad to something a bit special; and the fat in a steak keeps it moist and juicy when cooked.

- Fat adds texture, improving the mouthfeel of dish: it has an almost unifying or binding effect, holding the various components of a dish together. Foods fried in oil develop a crisp outer coating and crunch. Butter contributes to the flakiness of pastry, the rise and crumb of a cake and the layers of a croissant, while olive oil adds chewiness to a bread dough and succulence to roast fish.

- Fat contributes to visual appeal: it lends a golden colour to fried and baked foods; adds gloss to a chocolate sauce or mayonnaise; and helps retain the colour of herbs, chillies and vegetables in preserves.

- Fat plays an important role in nutrient absorption, especially fat-soluble vitamins: beta-carotene in carrots or spinach and lycopene found in tomatoes cannot be absorbed without the help of fat.

- Fat is crucial in baking, helping to leaven as well as lending flavour and moisture.

Oil

Some oils are better suited to cooking than others. Cooking oils should be stable at high temperatures, which is determined by the 'smoke point' – the temperature at which an oil starts to break down. Oils with a high smoke point are best for frying, baking, sautéing and roasting, while those with a low smoke point are good for dressings, sauces, salsas and dips (see individual oils, below). The choice can be overwhelming, so here are my go-tos.

Extra Virgin Olive Oil

My go-to for everything from dressings and dips, to shallow-frying, roasting and baking. Extra virgin olive oil (EVOO) is at the heart of the Mediterranean diet and its flavour, like that of wine, varies depending on where it comes from – its terroir and climate. A good extra virgin olive oil has an aroma of fresh olives, is deep green with a distinctive fruity, grassy or peppery flavour; it shouldn't smell or taste sour or stale as this is a sign of oxidation.

Extra virgin is the finest grade of olive oil made from the first cold pressing of the olives and has a low acidity rate (under 1 per cent). Pure olive oil is a mixture of extra virgin olive oil and refined olive oil and loses much of its antioxidant content through processing. It pays to check the label before buying EVOO as some oils labelled extra virgin may contain refined olive oil. A good-quality oil will often mention the harvest or pressing date of the olives.

For many years I avoided cooking with EVOO believing it wasn't heat stable. However, recent research has concluded that it is more heat stable than once thought, especially when compared with refined oils, thanks to its high antioxidant level. Its smoke point is around 190°C/375°F, while studies suggest the optimal temperature for shallow-frying is around 180°C/365°F. Baking and roasting are fine too, although try to avoid cooking it for long periods as this can cause chemical changes in the oil. I stick to a good-quality, average-priced extra virgin for shallow-frying, roasting and baking and splash out on a high-end one for dressings and dips, or for drizzling over soup or roast veg.

Health benefits

- Rich in the monounsaturated fat oleic acid (omega-9) thought to reduce inflammation in the body, which is a key driver behind many chronic diseases, including cancer, heart disease, type 2 diabetes, arthritis and metabolic syndrome.
- Beneficial source of immune-, skin- and eye-supporting vitamin E as well as vitamin K, which aids wound healing and blood clotting. High in many beneficial, free radical-fighting antioxidants.
- Promotes cognitive health, reduces depression, improves mood and may reduce the risk of Alzheimer's.
- Protects the heart by improving levels of beneficial HDL cholesterol and reducing oxidation of bad LDL cholesterol. Reduces the risk of strokes and high blood pressure.

Walnut & Hazelnut Oils

Deep, rich and nutty in flavour, these are my favourite nut oils. They are perfect for adding a final flourish to lentil, pasta and grain dishes, salads, or roast vegetables, soups, dips and stews. I use them in dressings for hearty salads of mixed leaves, beans, lentils or grains. The beauty of these oils is that they suit sweet dishes as well as savoury and are delicious drizzled over pancakes or used in mousses, cakes, biscuits and bakes.

These oils have a low smoke point (see page 22), so are best not used in cooking; they can become bitter if heated. Try to buy the best you can afford as nut oils vary greatly in quality and look for cold-pressed versions for peak nutty flavour. These oils are prone to oxidation, so try to buy them in small, dark glass bottles and keep an eye on the use-by date. You can store them in the fridge, too.

Health benefits

- Provide healthy amounts of monounsaturated and polyunsaturated fat with small amounts of saturated fat (see Nuts, page 36). Their good ratio of omega-6 to omega-3 helps to keep inflammation in check.

Hemp Seed Oil

I love the deep, nutty taste of this robust-flavoured seed oil, especially in salad dressings and drizzled over dips, grain, bean and rice salads and roast vegetables. Most hemp oil is unrefined and cold-pressed, so is best suited to uncooked dishes. It can be lightly heated, but since it has a low smoke point it becomes unstable when over-heated for long periods, which affects both its flavour and health benefits.

Health benefits
- A polyunsaturated fat providing a beneficial ratio of omega-3 to omega-6 fatty acids, found to reduce the risk of many chronic diseases (see page 9).
- Benefits the health and condition of the skin, hair and nails.

Coconut Oil

Depending on who you talk to, coconut oil is either revered or damned. This controversial oil has been making waves for some time, largely due to its high saturated fat content (around 82 per cent). Those for coconut oil argue that not all saturated fats are created equal. Solid at room temperature like butter and ghee, coconut oil is highly stable when heated and is perfect for shallow-frying, sautéing and stir-frying at high temperatures. Look for extra virgin pure coconut oil as this will be the best quality and unrefined.

Health benefits
- Features medium-chain saturated fatty acids that have antiviral, antifungal and antibacterial properties and may play a protective role in heart health.
- Medium-chain fatty acids are converted by the liver into energy and not stored as fat, suggesting that coconut oil may help weight loss.
- Contains significant levels of lauric acid, found to increase levels of beneficial HDL cholesterol.

Toasted Sesame Oil

A splash of toasted sesame seed oil at the end of cooking gives a final flourish to stir-fries, roasted vegetables and noodle dishes. It is not particularly heat stable, so avoid stir-frying with it, but add to Asian-style dressings.

Health benefits
- Rich in monounsaturated and polyunsaturated fat and low in saturates.
- A good source of vitamins B and E, calcium, magnesium and zinc.

Cold-pressed Rapeseed Oil

Once praised for its low saturated fat content, the tables have turned on rapeseed oil. Most rapeseed oil comes from genetically modified crops and is highly refined during processing, which diminishes any health attributes and can lead to some trans fats. But for me, unrefined, cold-pressed rapeseed oil produced from non-GM crops is a good light oil for mayonnaise and dressings. It can be lightly heated but avoid high temperatures or prolonged cooking.

Health benefits
- Cold-pressed rapeseed is not as highly processed as regular rapeseed, enabling it to retain nutrients such as vitamins E and K.
- Studies show it may boost levels of beneficial HDL cholesterol.

Give it a miss...
- Trans fats/partially hydrogenated fats
- Hydrogenated oils
- Refined, highly processed oils – soy, most rapeseed, vegetable and sunflower

How to Store Oil

Store oils in a cool, dark place as they are prone to spoiling, turning rancid or oxidizing if kept too warm or in direct sunlight. This is especially relevant to oils not used on a daily basis, such as nut oils, which can be kept in the fridge. Dark glass or tin, rather than plastic, is preferable with a tightly sealed lid.

Meat & Poultry

You don't need to give up meat when eating the right-fat way. Meat is a source of saturated fat, but it is also a good source of protein, omega-3 fatty acids, B vitamins and iron. If you do eat meat, go for quality – grass-fed, pasture-raised and/or free-range and/or organic – whenever possible. Meat from grass-fed cows is more expensive, but the time has come – from an environmental, health and economic perspective – for meat to be eaten in smaller quantities and only occasionally – once or twice a week, almost as a treat. This is a complex issue and there isn't space to cover it in detail here, but there appears to be positive evidence that cows raised primarily on pasture, using traditional farming methods may have a positive impact on the environment and our health.

There is much to say about chicken production and the huge gulf between the different methods of farming, but the single overriding message is to buy organic whenever possible. Even the term 'free range' can be misleading and open to interpretation. Organic chickens are raised to high welfare standards – do look for Soil Association approval.

Health benefits
- The meat from grass-fed cows provides up to three times more omega-3 fatty acids than that from intensively reared, grain-fed cattle, as well as higher concentrations of antioxidants, minerals and vitamins, including vitamins A and E.
- Free-range pork is said to contain higher levels of vitamin E and iron.
- Organic, pasture-fed lamb provides at least 25 per cent more omega-3 than conventionally fed lamb, and has lower levels of fat overall.
- Organic chicken contains higher levels of omega-3, particularly those fed an omega-3 enriched diet.

Give it a miss...
- Meat from intensively farmed, grain-fed cows
- Intensively reared, non-organic pork, lamb and chicken

Fish & Shellfish

When it comes to eating right fats, oily fish comes top of the list thanks to its impressive levels of omega-3. The World Health Organization (WHO) recommends eating oily fish twice a week, including salmon, mackerel, herring, pilchards, sardines or trout. Tuna has been taken off the recommended list as it has been found to contain higher levels of mercury than other fish.

White fish and shellfish also provide omega-3, albeit in smaller amounts, and good options include sea bass, bream, turbot and halibut as well as mussels, oysters, clams, squid and crab. Lower in fat are plaice (flounder), cod, haddock, red mullet (snapper), gurnard and tilapia. The current recommendation is one portion of white fish a week.

Don't discount canned fish. Canned red salmon, sardines, pilchards, mackerel and anchovies make perfect storecupboard staples and the canning process does not appear to diminish their omega-3 content (apart from tuna). Cheap, nutritious and versatile, canned fish can be turned into a quick pasta sauce or fishcakes, stirred into rice or grains, the base of a pie or salad, the filling for an omelette or a topping for toast. The small bones in canned salmon, pilchards and sardines are also a good source of calcium.

Not all fish has a clean bill of health and we need to be mindful of sustainability – check the Marine Stewardship Council (MSC) list – and whether the fish is farmed or wild. It is not only the environmental impact of farmed fish that is in question, the nutritional quality of farmed versus wild has been under the spotlight too. Wild fish, particularly salmon and trout, have been found to have higher levels of omega-3 than farmed.

When buying fish, it should be at the peak of freshness. The skin and eyes of whole fish should be bright, clear and glowing; fillets and steaks should be firm and moist and not mushy; the shells of mussels and clams shut (or closed when tapped). Oily fish becomes a lot stronger in flavour if more than a day old because of its high ratio of fat, so it pays to buy wisely.

Health benefits

- Omega-3 fatty acids have been found to boost brain function and reduce cognitive impairment. There appears to be a link between omega-3 from oily fish and a slower rate of age-related mental decline, even for people with a high risk of Alzheimer's. The fatty acid is crucial for brain development and growth in babies and young children. For other benefits see page 9.

Give it a miss...

- Fish and seafood on the endangered list
- Farmed fish, including salmon and trout
- Canned or flaked tuna (or other fish) in vegetable, soya or other refined oil and canned pink salmon

Dairy

There are decisions to be made when buying milk beyond whether it is whole, semi-skimmed or skimmed. The environment and animal welfare are two major considerations. At one end of the spectrum are large-scale operations with dairy herds kept indoors and fed largely a grain-based diet and at the opposite end are small-scale organic farms where cows are fed mainly grass or forage, supplemented during the colder winter months with cereals or pulses. What is striking is that not only does there appear to be environmental and welfare benefits to grass-fed dairy cows, there are health benefits, too.

Whole milk has had a bad rap over the years, particularly for its saturated fat and cholesterol content so it may be a surprise to learn whole milk has been found to be a heart-friendly food. A recent study found that grass-fed cows produce milk with five times as much of an unsaturated fat called conjugated linoleic acid (CLA) than cows fed processed grains. Studies suggest CLAs may protect the heart, reducing the risk of a heart attack, stroke, type 2 diabetes

and weight gain, especially harmful visceral fat around the waist, and certain cancers. The fat in the milk also plays the role of carrier, transporting fat-soluble vitamins and essential fatty acids around the body.

All dairy products start from the same base – milk – and it is truly amazing to think that this versatile, nutritious food makes such an incredible number of by-products, including butter, cream, crème fraîche, yogurt and cheese – about three moderate servings a day is recommended. Similarly, the fat content of dairy products is equally diverse, ranging from zero up to 80 per cent. Like wine and olive oil, the taste of milk is influenced by soil and climate, along with the diet of the cows. These nuances of flavour affect the milk by-products. It comes as no surprise, then, that butter and cheese from grass-fed dairy cows show similar health benefits to their milk. Additionally, butter from grass-fed herbs has been found to have higher levels of unsaturated fat than regular butter.

Health benefits
- Grass-fed/organic cows produce milk with a higher ratio of anti-inflammatory omega-3 to omega-6 fatty acids, as well as higher concentrations of vitamins and antioxidants. There is further evidence to suggest that organic whole milk contains a higher proportion of omega-3 than regular full-fat milk, and significantly higher than semi-skimmed and skimmed milk.
- While vitamin and calcium levels are very similar, partly due to fortification, there is an argument that fat-soluble, immunity-supporting vitamins such as A, D, K and B vitamins may be better absorbed when from whole milk. Vitamin D helps our bodies absorb calcium.
- Milk provides high-quality protein and calcium. Calcium may influence the impact of saturated fat found in dairy on heart disease.
- Raw milk/cheese are rich in microbes that boost gut health.
- Iodine, a mineral required to make thyroid hormones, found in milk is responsible for growth and metabolism. Studies show a link between low iodine levels in mothers and reduced cognitive performance in their children.

Yogurt (live)

Yogurt (and kefir) not only provide the same range of health benefits as other dairy products, these fermented foods also contain probiotic bacteria that support digestion and gut health. Buy plain or natural yogurt with live, active, gut-supporting cultures, such as *Bifidobacteria* and *Lactobacillus*. Pasteurization is said to kill the good bacteria in live yogurt so it is vital to choose a brand that adds cultures after heat treatment. Check the label for verification.

In these recipes, I have used Greek-style plain unsweetened yogurt as I prefer its rich, creamy flavour and texture. It can be used instead of cream in cooking without splitting if added at the end and warmed through with care. Low-fat yogurts contain additives, thickening agents, fillers and often sugar to make up for the lack of fat – when it comes to yogurt, less is generally more.

Health benefits
- Rich in protein and probiotic or live cultures that benefit the digestive system, easing conditions such as irritable bowel syndrome (IBS) and supporting the immune system.
- Rich in minerals, including calcium, magnesium and potassium for healthy bones, as well as B vitamins for energy.
- May reduce the risk of type 2 diabetes and benefit heart health.

Give it a miss...
- Processed cheese spreads, imitation cheese with additives and low-fat dairy products
- Butter alternatives/spreads and spreads containing trans/partially hydrogenated fat
- Sweetened yogurts
- Soft-scoop ice cream

Eggs

Eggs are the complete package: nutritious, versatile and inexpensive. A few years back eggs fell out of favour due to their high cholesterol content. Yet, following the discovery that dietary cholesterol in eggs has little influence on levels of bad LDL cholesterol, they are back. In fact, eggs have since been found to raise levels of good HDL cholesterol. As a result, previous guidelines on egg consumption have been removed and the general consensus is that eating up to three eggs a day is perfectly healthy.

When buying eggs, choose organic free-range for both animal welfare and nutritional reasons. Eggs from free-range chickens have been found to contain higher amounts of vitamins A, D, E as well as omega-3 – their fat content means that these nutrients are better absorbed. The recipes suggest using eggs fortified with omega-3, which come from chickens fed a diet supplemented with omega-3 enriched flaxseeds, a definite benefit if you are vegetarian and avoid eating oily fish.

Health benefits
- Rich in high-quality protein and healthy fats, eggs provide a wide range of minerals, including iodine, zinc, iron, copper, phosphorus and selenium as well as vitamins A, some Bs, D, K and folate.
- Omega-3 enriched eggs provide up to five time more of the essential fatty acid than regular eggs.
- Rich in choline, found to reduce the risk of heart disease and stroke and essential for brain development.

Give it a miss...
- Barn/happy eggs

Nuts & Seeds

Breakfast wouldn't be breakfast without nuts and seeds. It's not only their nutritional benefits that appeal, but their versatility and ability to add flavour and texture to both sweet and savoury dishes. Many people avoid eating nuts and seeds due to their high fat content, but they provide largely good fats with relatively small amounts of saturated fat. Interestingly, nuts may stimulate our metabolism, encouraging the body to burn more calories!

Nuts and seeds make a great, nutrient-dense snack, keeping us fuller for longer thanks to their slow-releasing energy. A handful a day has been found to reduce harmful LDL cholesterol thus reducing the risk of heart disease, keep blood sugar levels steady and possibly reduce cognitive decline, particularly in the elderly.

Nut and seed milks, and other plant-based dairy alternatives, make a valuable nutritious alternative to dairy milk, especially if fortified with calcium and vitamins B12 and D – some also contain an extra boost of omega-3.

You can soak nuts before eating to increase their digestibility, but it is not essential. However, linseeds and chia seeds should be soaked first as they can pass through the body without being properly digested. When soaked in water, these seeds become gelatinous and are a good alternative to eggs in baking.

To keep nuts and seeds fresh, as their oils can become rancid, buy them in usable amounts and store in an airtight container in a cool, dark place or in the fridge. You can also store them in the freezer – there is no need to defrost them before use.

Toasting Nuts & Seeds

Many recipes in this book recommend toasting nuts or seeds. This adds another layer of flavour and gives them extra crunch. Oven-roast nuts and seeds to achieve an even toasting, but if you only need a small amount, then toast them in a dry frying pan. Be mindful of not over-toasting them as they can easily burn, which makes them taste bitter and damages their heat-sensitive good fats.

- Preheat the oven to 180°C/350°F/gas mark 4. Spread the nuts or seeds out on a baking tray lined with baking (parchment) paper. Toast for 5–10 minutes for seeds and 12–20 minutes for nuts, turning or stirring halfway to cook them evenly. Timings can vary depending on the size and variety of nut or seed, but they should be light golden when ready. Remove from the oven and transfer to a plate to cool and crisp up further. Store in an airtight container for up to 5 days.

Health benefits
- Nuts and seeds are a rich source of protein, fibre, vitamin, minerals, antioxidants and phytochemicals.
- New research has linked walnuts with improved memory and cognitive processing due to their omega-3 content, while Brazil nuts are one of the richest sources of immune-supporting selenium. Almonds are one of the most nutritionally dense nuts with impressive levels of magnesium, potassium and vitamin E.
- Flaxseeds, chia, hemp and pumpkin seeds are rich in omega-3 as are hazelnuts, pecans and walnuts. Additionally, flaxseeds are rich in lignans, antioxidants linked with a reduced risk of certain cancers.
- Hemp seeds are one of the few plant foods that are a complete protein, containing all nine essential amino acids. They are also a perfect balance of essential fatty acids.

Not Forgetting... Avocados

How could I not mention avocados? This nutrient-dense fruit has been chastised in the past for its high fat content, but most of this is heart-protective oleic acid. Despite their numerous health benefits, it pays to eat avocados in moderate amounts, particularly from an environmental perspective. It seems our ferocious appetite for avocados has had a negative impact on the environment due to land clearing and an over-demand for precious water.

Health benefits
- Avocados provide antioxidants vitamin E and beta-carotene. They are also a good source of iron, copper, potassium and B vitamins as well as beneficial amounts of fibre.
- Rich in the monounsaturated fat, oleic acid, which reduces inflammation in the body, benefits the heart, reduces high blood pressure and the risk of stroke and type 2 diabetes.

Avocado Oil

This vibrant green oil is a bit pricey, but a splash is a great way to add flavour to cooked seafood, vegetables, rice, beans and salads. Pressed from the pulp of avocados, the oil has quite a strong, distinct flavour, so be mindful of the amount you use or combine with other oils if you find it too dominant. It is highly versatile and stable enough to use in cooking with one of the highest smoke points, so perfect for frying, baking and roasting, and special enough to use in salad dressings.

Health benefits
- Rich in monounsaturated fats, particularly heart-healthy oleic acid.
- Effective at increasing beneficial HDL cholesterol as well as reducing high blood pressure and the symptoms of arthritis.
- High in antioxidants, particularly lutein, which supports eye health.
- Provides vitamin E, improving skin health and an effective moisturiser.

01
Rise 'n' Shine

Cherry Chia Breakfast Pots

Saturated Fat 7.5g
Unsaturated Fat 12.3g
Calories 386kcal
per serving

Frozen dark cherries come ready stoned and are super convenient, especially when fresh cherries are out of season. If you have difficulty in finding them, any frozen berry, or combination of berries, would make a good alternative. These fruit pots are thickened with chia seeds, which although tiny provide a gamut of nutrients from plant-based omega-3 to protein and fibre, and more besides. Most of the preparation can be done the night before to save you precious time in the morning.

Serves 4
Prep: 15 minutes, plus soaking

2 rounded tbsp chia seeds

5 soft dried dates, chopped

300ml/10 fl oz/1¼ cups organic whole milk or dairy-free alternative, such as nut or oat milk

225g/8 oz frozen dark cherries or other berries, defrosted

1 tsp ground cinnamon, plus extra for sprinkling

200g/7 oz/scant 1 cup Greek-style yogurt or dairy-free alternative

4 tbsp good-quality granola (see page 44)

40g/1½ oz/generous ⅓ cup pecans, roughly chopped

Soak the chia seeds and dates in the milk for at least 1 hour, or overnight if possible. Defrost the cherries in the fridge at the same time.

Put the chia mixture in a blender with the cherries and cinnamon, until smooth and creamy. Spoon into four glasses or bowls and top with the yogurt, granola, pecans, the reserved cherries and a sprinkling of cinnamon.

Walnut, Coconut & Cinnamon Granola

Saturated Fat 7.1g
Unsaturated Fat 17.3g
Calories 368kcal
per 68g serving

Making your own granola gives you the freedom to choose what you put into it and to optimize the use of good fats with nutritious nuts, seeds and grains. Ready-made granolas can sneak in palm or hydrogenated oils and can be overly sugary and surprisingly salty. This one uses extra virgin coconut oil and jumbo porridge oats, but you could experiment with different oils and grains, such as extra virgin olive oil and rye, buckwheat or quinoa.

Makes: about 10 servings

Prep: 10 minutes

Cook: 45 minutes

5 tbsp extra virgin coconut oil

5 tbsp maple syrup

225g/8 oz/2⅓ cups jumbo porridge oats

75g/2½ oz/½ cup mixed seeds, including sesame, sunflower and pumpkin

100g/3½ oz/scant 1 cup walnuts, broken into pieces

75g/2½ oz/¾ cup pecan halves, broken into pieces

1 tbsp ground cinnamon

pinch of sea salt

4 tbsp hemp seeds

Greek-style yogurt, milk or dairy-free alternatives and fresh or dried fruit, to serve

Preheat the oven to 150°C fan/170°C/325°F/gas mark 3. Line 2 baking trays (sheets) with baking (parchment) paper.

Warm the coconut oil and maple syrup in a small saucepan over a low heat.

Meanwhile put the oats, seeds, walnuts, pecans, cinnamon and salt in a large mixing bowl and stir well.

Pour the oil mixture into the bowl and stir until mixed together. Tip the granola onto the prepared baking trays and spread out evenly. Toast for 35–40 minutes, turning every 15 minutes and swapping the trays round in the oven, until golden and crisp. The granola will crisp up further once cooled. When cool, stir in the hemp seeds and store in a lidded jar for up to 2 weeks.

Chocolate & Hazelnut Smoothie Bowls

Saturated Fat 5.2g
Unsaturated Fat 26.6g
Calories 551kcal
per serving

Hemp is very much the ingredient of the moment, with its winning combination of plant-based omega-3, protein, magnesium, potassium and zinc. The seeds also make an excellent creamy, dairy-free milk when blended with water, and forms the base of this hazelnut, chocolate and avocado smoothie bowl.

Serves 2
Prep: 10 minutes, plus soaking
Cook: 5 minutes

5 soft dried dates

3 tbsp hemp seeds, plus extra to serve

25g/1 oz/$\frac{1}{5}$ cup hazelnuts

1 ripe avocado, halved, stoned and flesh scooped out

1 tbsp raw cacao powder

$\frac{1}{2}$ tsp ground cinnamon, plus extra to serve

150g/5$\frac{1}{2}$ oz strawberries, hulled and halved or seasonal fruit of choice

Soak the dates for 20 minutes in hot water until softened. At the same time, soak the hemp seeds in 150ml/5$\frac{1}{2}$ fl oz/ scant $\frac{2}{3}$ cup water.

Meanwhile, toast the hazelnuts in a large, dry frying pan (skillet) for 5 minutes, turning the nuts occasionally, until they start to colour. Leave to cool and roughly chop.

Drain and roughly chop the dates. Put them in a blender with the avocado, cacao powder, hemp milk and cinnamon and blend until smooth and creamy. Spoon into two small bowls and top with the strawberries, hazelnuts, hemp seeds and a little extra cinnamon. Serve straightaway or chill briefly.

Avocado with Trout Tartare on Rye

Saturated Fat 2.7g
Unsaturated Fat 11.5g
Calories 233kcal
per serving

Just the thing when you are looking for a light and rejuvenating breakfast, avocados are rich in monounsaturated fat and are thought to help reduce levels of harmful LDL cholesterol in the blood. Prepare the trout tartare no longer than 20 minutes before serving as the lime juice will start to 'cook' the fish.

Serves 4
Prep: 10 minutes

4 slices dark, seeded rye bread

2 small ripe avocados, halved and stoned

juice of 1 lime

2 tsp good-quality mayonnaise, preferably homemade
(see page 113)

1 large handful radish or broccoli sprouts

For the trout tartare

100g/3½ oz smoked trout, cut into small pieces

1 small cucumber, quartered lengthways, deseeded and diced

8 radishes, diced

1 tbsp diced red onion

juice of 1 lime

freshly ground black pepper

First make the trout tartare. Put all the ingredients in a bowl and fold gently until combined. Set aside while you prepare the rest of the dish.

Lightly toast the rye bread.

While the bread is toasting, prepare the avocado. Peel off the skin, cut into long thin slices and squeeze over the lime juice to prevent it discolouring.

Spread the mayonnaise over the toasted rye and top with the avocado, slightly mashing it with the back of a fork. Spoon the trout tartare on top and finish with a sprinkling of sprouts. Season with pepper – you are unlikely to need any extra salt as the smoked trout is already quite salty. Serve immediately.

Three-Nut Butter & Apples on Toast

Saturated Fat 5.8g
Unsaturated Fat 15.3g
Calories 443kcal
per serving

Making your own nut butter allows you to use your favourite nuts and avoid additives, such as palm oil, sugar and salt, that can creep into shop-bought alternatives. Both the nut butter and apple compote can be made in advance to save you time in the morning. They make a fine partnership on toast and are also excellent on brioche or pancakes.

Serves 4
Prep: 20 minutes, plus cooling
Cook: 10 minutes

4–8 slices seedy wholewheat bread, depending on size
Greek-style yogurt, to serve

For the nut butter
(makes 200g/7 oz)
100g/3½ oz/¾ cup unsalted peanuts
50g/1¾ oz/scant ½ cup cashew nuts
50g/1¾ oz/scant ½ cup hazelnuts
1 tbsp organic cold-pressed rapeseed oil
pinch of sea salt

For the apple compote
4 red apples, cored and chopped, skin left on
squeeze of lemon juice
½ tsp mixed spice

First make the nut butter. Preheat the oven to 150°C fan/170°C/325°F/gas mark 3. Line a large baking tray (sheet) with baking (parchment) paper.

Spread the peanuts, cashews and hazelnuts out on the baking tray and cook for 15 minutes, turning halfway through cooking, until starting to colour and smell toasted. Leave to cool. Tip the nuts into a mini food processor or blender. Add the oil and salt and blend until almost smooth and creamy. You may need to scrape the mixture down once or twice so everything blends evenly. Scoop into a lidded jar – it will keep for up to 2 weeks in the fridge.

Meanwhile for the compote, put the apples in a saucepan with the lemon juice, 3 tablespoons of water and the mixed spice. Cook over a medium-low heat, partially covered, for 5–8 minutes until the apples are tender. Lightly mash with the back of a fork to break up the apples.

When ready to serve, toast the bread. Spread over a spoonful of the nut butter, heap the apples on top and finish with a good spoonful of yogurt.

Oat & Flaxseed Pancakes
with Salmon & Crispy Capers

Saturated Fat 12.2g
Unsaturated Fat 7g
Calories 416kcal
per serving

Oats are not particularly known for their fat-friendly status, yet they are one of the most nutrient-dense grains you can eat as they are a good source of complex carbs, fibre, protein and polyunsaturated and monounsaturated fats. As an added bonus, this brunch provides beneficial amounts of omega-3 from the flaxseeds and smoked salmon.

Serves 4
Prep: 15 minutes
Cook: 20 minutes

100g/3½ oz/1 cup jumbo porridge oats

a large pinch sea salt

½ tsp bicarbonate of soda (baking soda)

1 tbsp milled flaxseeds

2 eggs, preferably omega-3 enriched

125g/3½ oz/½ cup plus 1 tbsp Greek-style yogurt

1 tbsp lemon juice, plus extra for squeezing over

2 tbsp melted butter, plus extra for cooking

To serve

4 tbsp crème fraîche (sour cream)

finely grated zest and juice of 1 small unwaxed lemon

splash of extra virgin olive oil

2 tbsp non-pareille capers, drained and patted dry

100g/3½ oz smoked salmon or trout

1 tbsp snipped chives

freshly ground black pepper

To make the pancakes, mix together the dry ingredients in a bowl. Crack the eggs into a separate mixing bowl and whisk in the yogurt, lemon juice and melted butter. Gradually whisk the dry ingredients into the eggs to make a smooth, thick batter. Set aside briefly while you prepare the serving ingredients.

Mix together the crème fraîche and lemon juice and zest in a bowl and set aside.

Heat a splash of oil in a large frying pan (skillet), add the capers and fry over a medium heat until crisp and starting to turn golden – take care as they can spit a bit. Drain on kitchen paper and set aside. Wipe the pan clean with kitchen paper.

Reheat the frying pan over a medium heat. Add enough butter to lightly coat the base and when melted, add 3 tablespoons of the batter per pancake – you should be able to cook three at a time. Cook for about 2 minutes on each side until golden. Drain on kitchen paper and keep warm in a low oven while you make the rest – the batter should make 10–12.

To serve, divide the pancakes between four serving plates and top with a good spoonful of the crème fraîche mixture, then the salmon. Season with black pepper and scatter over the chives and crispy capers.

Roast Mushroom & Tomato Brunch

Saturated Fat 4.5g
Unsaturated Fat 10.2g
Calories 265kcal
per serving

I love a meal that can be cooked in one roasting tin and brunch is the perfect time for this type of dish as, quite frankly, the simpler the better. It's fascinating how some ingredients enhance the nutritional value of others; roasting the tomatoes with oil, for instance, amplifies the availability of lycopene in the tomatoes. This antioxidant helps protect the health of the eyes and the gut. The brunch comes with a Parsley Relish (see page 65), but it is equally good with a sprinkling of Dukkah (see page 106).

Serves 4
Prep: 10 minutes
Cook: 40 minutes

3 tbsp extra virgin olive oil

400g/14 oz new potatoes, scrubbed, halved or quartered if large

4 large portobello mushrooms, stalks removed

15g/½ oz/generous 1 tbsp butter

1 large garlic clove

300g/10½ oz small vine-ripened tomatoes

4 eggs, preferably omega-3 enriched

dried chilli flakes (optional)

sea salt and black pepper

rocket (arugula) leaves and Parsley Relish (see page 65), to serve (optional)

Preheat the oven to 180°C fan/200°C/400°F/gas mark 6.

Pour 1 tablespoon of the oil into a large roasting tin (pan). Add the potatoes and roll them around to coat in the oil. Brush a second tablespoon of the oil over the base of each mushroom. Place the mushrooms in the tin, cap-side down, and top each one with a small knob of butter. Finely grate the garlic over each one and season with salt and pepper. Cover the tin with foil. Bake for 20 minutes until the mushrooms have softened slightly.

Remove the foil, turn the potatoes and add the tomatoes. Crack an egg into a cup and carefully pour it on top of one of the mushrooms so it sits in the hollow. Repeat with the rest of the eggs. Return to the oven and cook, uncovered, for a further 18–20 minutes or until the white of the eggs is just set. Serve, sprinkled with chilli flakes and the Parsley Relish, if liked, and with rocket leaves on the side.

Poached Eggs with Gomashio & Spinach

Omega-3 eggs come from hens fed a diet containing flaxseed, while some producers also add fish-sourced omega-3 to the feed. Eggs, fortified or not, make a great start to the day and are packed with vitamins, minerals, protein and healthy fats. In this super-simple breakfast, they are served with gomashio, the Japanese seasoning made with sesame seeds and sea salt to which I've also added nori flakes.

Serves 4
Prep: 10 minutes
Cook: 10 minutes

1 tbsp extra virgin olive oil

200g/7 oz baby spinach leaves, washed

juice of ½ lemon

4 large eggs, preferably omega-3 enriched

freshly ground black pepper

buttered, toasted seeded wholemeal (whole wheat) bread, to serve

For the gomashio

2 tsp toasted sesame seeds

2 tsp sea salt flakes

1 tsp nori flakes

Mix together all the ingredients for the gomashio and set aside.

Heat a large, deep sauté pan over a medium heat. Add the oil and spinach and a splash of water and stir-fry for 2–3 minutes or until wilted. Season with salt and pepper and squeeze over the lemon juice. Tip the spinach into a warm bowl and cover to keep warm.

Wipe the pan clean and three-quarters fill with just-boiled water from a kettle. Place the pan over a low heat and swirl the water (you could also add a splash of vinegar). Crack the eggs, one at a time, into a cup, then tip them into the pan. Poach the eggs for 3–4 minutes until the whites are set but the yolks remain runny. Remove with a slotted spoon and drain on kitchen paper.

Spoon the spinach onto four plates and top with an egg, a sprinkling of gomashio and a grinding of black pepper. Serve with buttered toast on the side.

Scrambled Tofu on Rye

Saturated Fat 9.5g
Unsaturated Fat 12.3g
Calories 350kcal
per serving

The first time I made this it was a revelation – so tasty, so quick and a brand-new way to enjoy tofu. I've kept it simple with the flavourings using turmeric and nutritional yeast flakes, but there is lots of scope to experiment with herbs, spices and various vegetable additions. Nutritional yeast flakes can be bought in tubs in supermarkets or health food shops and are a good source of vitamin B12. The tofu is scrambled in avocado oil as I had some to hand. It is said to be one of the few extra virgin plant oils that can withstand heat without losing its heart-friendly health benefits, but extra virgin olive oil or coconut oil are both good alternatives.

Serves 4
Prep: 10 minutes
Cook: 5 minutes

400g/14 oz firm tofu, drained well and cut into quarters
2½ tbsp avocado oil, extra virgin olive oil or coconut oil
1 tsp ground turmeric
2 tbsp nutritional yeast flakes
sea salt and black pepper

To serve

4 slices dark, seeded rye bread
good-quality mayonnaise (see page 113), butter or spread of choice
sriracha sauce
8 vine-ripened tomatoes, quartered

Squeeze the tofu in your hands to get rid of any excess water – it doesn't matter if it breaks up slightly – then pat dry with kitchen paper. Place in a bowl and mash with the back of a fork to break the tofu into small pieces.

Heat the oil over a medium-low heat, then add the tofu, turmeric and yeast flakes. Turn with a spatula until everything is evenly combined, then continue to stir for 3–5 minutes to warm through. Season with salt and pepper to taste.

Meanwhile, toast the rye bread and spread with mayo, butter or your spread of choice. Place on four plates and spoon the scrambled tofu on top. Serve with a drizzle of sriracha sauce and tomatoes on the side.

Mozzarella, Tomato & Sardines on Toast

Saturated Fat 9.4g
Unsaturated Fat 14.9g
Calories 505kcal
per serving

Canned fish is often seen as the poor relation to its fresh cousin, yet it can be such an asset in the right-fat store cupboard. Quick, fuss-free and economical, canned sardines, mackerel, pilchards, salmon and anchovies (not tuna unfortunately, which loses its good fats during processing) are an important source of protein and omega-3. What's more, the small bones are an excellent source of calcium.

Serves 1

Prep: 10 minutes

Cook: 5 minutes

135g/4¾ oz can sardines in olive oil (about 90g/3¼ oz drained weight), drained

2 vine-ripened tomatoes, deseeded and diced

¼ tsp hot smoked paprika

squeeze of lemon juice

2 slices seeded wholewheat bread

½ tsp good-quality mayonnaise (see page 113)

40g/1½ oz/½ cup mozzarella, drained and torn into pieces

freshly ground black pepper

Preheat the grill to high.

While the grill is heating up, put the sardines in a bowl with the tomatoes and paprika. Add a squeeze of lemon juice and season with pepper.

Toast one side of each slice of bread until golden. Turn over the bread and lightly spread the untoasted side with mayonnaise. Spoon the sardine mixture on top, spreading it out to the edges of the bread, then scatter over the mozzarella. Grill for 5 minutes or until the mozzarella has melted and started to colour. Finish with another grinding of black pepper and serve.

02

Small
Plates

Coconut, Carrot & Lentil Soup

Saturated Fat 6.1g
Unsaturated Fat 1.5g
Calories 290kcal
per serving

Warming and sustaining, this filling golden soup uses coconut drinking milk for a creamy texture – be sure to buy an unsweetened variety. Fibre-rich lentils, ginger and spices all have a reputation for improving and benefiting the health of our gut. This dish also comes with a beetroot raita that adds great colour as well as extra nutritional value, including iron, potassium and fibre.

Serves 4
Prep: 20 minutes
Cook: 30 minutes

1 tbsp extra virgin coconut oil, butter or ghee
1 large onion, roughly chopped
1 celery stick, thinly sliced
3 carrots, sliced
2 garlic cloves, finely chopped
5cm/2 in piece fresh ginger, finely chopped
6 cardamom pods, split
1 tsp ground turmeric
2 bay leaves
175g/6 oz/1 cup split red lentils, rinsed well
800ml/28 fl oz/3½ cups vegetable stock
400ml/14 fl oz/1¾ cups unsweetened coconut drinking milk
1 tbsp garam masala
sea salt and black pepper

For the beetroot raita
100g/3½ oz/scant ½ cup Greek-style yogurt
1 large cooked beetroot (beet) in natural juice (not vinegar), drained and diced
juice of ½ lime, plus extra to serve
½ tsp nigella seeds

Heat a large saucepan over a medium heat. Add the oil and onion and cook, covered with a lid, for 5 minutes, until softened but not coloured. Add the celery, carrots, garlic, ginger, cardamom, turmeric and bay leaves, stir well, and cook for a further 2 minutes.

Add the lentils, stock and coconut milk and bring to the boil, then reduce the heat to low and simmer, partially covered, for 20 minutes or until the lentils are tender. Five minutes before the end of the cooking time, stir in the garam masala.

Meanwhile, mix together all the ingredients for the beetroot raita and season with salt and pepper.

Pick out the cardamom and bay leaves, then blend the soup using a stick blender until smooth. Season with salt and pepper and add a good squeeze of lime juice. Serve topped with the beetroot raita.

Mexican Pumpkin Seed Dip

Saturated Fat 2.7g
Unsaturated Fat 10.8g
Calories 322kcal
per serving

Inspired by a dish tried in a local Mexican restaurant, pumpkin seeds make a surprisingly good dip. They may be small and unassuming, but pumpkin seeds are a nutritional powerhouse, providing plant-based omega-3, protein, zinc and magnesium as well as iron, selenium and B vitamins.

Serves about 8
Prep: 15 minutes
Cook: 25 minutes

200g/7 oz/scant 1½ cups pumpkin seeds

4 vine-ripened tomatoes

2 garlic cloves, peeled

1 small onion, cut into wedges

3 tbsp extra virgin olive oil, plus extra for drizzling

juice 2 large limes

1 tsp dried chipotle flakes

2 handfuls coriander (cilantro) leaves, finely chopped

2 handfuls flat-leaf parsley leaves, finely chopped

sea salt and black pepper

8 corn tortillas, to serve

Toast the seeds in a large, deep sauté pan over a medium-low heat, turning them often, for 6–8 minutes until they start to pop and colour slightly. Leave to cool.

Blacken the tomatoes, garlic and onion in the large, dry sauté pan over a medium heat for 8–10 minutes, turning them occasionally, until charred in places. Leave to cool.

Set aside 1 tablespoon of pumpkin seeds, then put the rest in a food processor with the charred vegetables, olive oil, lime juice, chipotle flakes and 3 tablespoons of water. Process to a course-textured dip, adding a splash more water if needed. Spoon into a serving bowl and stir in most of the herbs, leaving some to garnish, and season well with salt and pepper. Taste and add more water, lime juice and chipotle flakes if needed. Top with a drizzle of oil and the reserved seeds and herbs.

Just before serving, warm the tortillas in an oven preheated to 170°C/325°F/gas mark 3 for 5 minutes, turning once, or until crisp. Break into wedges and serve with the dip.

Puy Lentil, Orange & Sunflower Seed Salad with Walnut Oil Dressing

Saturated Fat 1.7g
Unsaturated Fat 13.6g
Calories 314kcal
per serving

Walnut oil has a warm, rich, nutty flavour that works beautifully with the lentils, red cabbage and celery in this salad. For optimum health and taste benefits – including impressive plant-sourced omega-3, monounsaturated fats and antioxidants – look for a good-quality cold-pressed walnut oil. This salad is also delicious with hemp seed oil and a smattering of crumbled Stilton or other blue cheese.

Serves 4
Prep: 15 minutes
Cook: 25 minutes

125g/4½ oz/½ cup plus 2 tbsp dried Puy lentils, rinsed
2 oranges
150g/5½ oz red cabbage, finely shredded
3 celery sticks, thinly sliced
2 spring onions (scallions), thinly sliced diagonally
100g/3½ oz baby kale leaves
2 handfuls flat-leaf parsley leaves, roughly chopped
2 tbsp toasted sunflower seeds

For the dressing
4 tbsp cold-pressed walnut oil or extra virgin hemp oil
1½ tbsp raw apple cider vinegar
1 tsp wholegrain mustard
1 tsp good-quality runny honey
sea salt and black pepper

Cook the lentils in a pan of boiling water for 20–25 minutes or until tender, then drain well and leave them to sit in the sieve while you prepare the rest of the salad.

Meanwhile, peel the oranges and remove any white outer pith. Place them on a plate and cut between the membranes to remove the segments.

Mix together all the ingredients for the dressing and season well with salt and pepper. Taste and add more oil, vinegar, mustard or honey if needed. Add any juice from the segmented oranges.

Tip the lentils into a large, shallow serving bowl and add the cabbage, celery and spring onions. Spoon over half the dressing and toss until combined. Add the orange segments, kale and parsley, toss gently and spoon over as much dressing as needed. Scatter over the sunflower seeds and serve.

Mushroom, Kale & Sweet Potato Hash with Dukkah

Saturated Fat 1.7g
Unsaturated Fat 8.5g
Calories 293kcal
per serving

One-pan meals are a blessing when you're in a rush, yet still want to eat something nutritious. The beauty of this dish is that it can be readily adapted depending on what you have to hand and is perfect for using up leftover bits and pieces in the fridge. The dukkah is a great way to up the good fat count. You can buy it ready made, but I've included a recipe on page 106 – it's always worth keeping a jar in the fridge to add an extra boost of flavour, texture and nutritional value.

Serves 4
Prep: 15 minutes
Cook: 30 minutes

3 tbsp extra virgin olive oil

300g/10⅓ oz chestnut (cremini) mushrooms, torn into pieces

125g/4½ oz kale, tough stalks removed, torn into small pieces

3 garlic cloves, finely chopped

4 large vine-ripened tomatoes, cut into chunks

400g/14 oz can chickpeas, drained

350g/12 oz cooked sweet potatoes, cut into chunks

1 tbsp harissa paste

juice of ½–1 lemon, to taste

sea salt and black pepper

Dukkah (see page 106) and hummus, to serve

Heat a large, deep sauté pan over a medium heat. Add the oil and mushrooms and fry for 10 minutes, stirring, until they start to colour and any liquid in the pan evaporates. Stir in the kale – you may need to do it a couple of batches – and cook for a further 2–3 minutes or until wilted.

Add the garlic and tomatoes and cook for 1 minute, then add the chickpeas and sweet potatoes. Stir gently until combined, then add the harissa and a splash of water. Cook for 5 minutes, stirring occasionally, and finish with a squeeze of lemon and salt and pepper. Taste and adjust the seasoning if you need to. Serve in large, shallow bowls with the dukkah sprinkled on top and a good spoonful of hummus.

Cauliflower Cheese Soup with Parsley Relish

Saturated Fat 10g
Unsaturated Fat 11g
Calories 400kcal
per serving

A celebration of dairy, this rich, creamy soup is not one to eat every day, but it makes the perfect comforting soup when it's cold outside. Choose a Cheddar cheese with a good robust flavour, preferably made with milk from grass-fed cows. This has been found to have a better balance of omega-3 and omega-6 fatty acids than regular milk. The parsley relish cuts through the richness of the soup, adding a touch of zing.

Serves 4
Prep: 20 minutes
Cook: 20 minutes

40g/1½ oz/3 tbsp butter

2 onions, roughly chopped

1 celery stick, thinly sliced

2 garlic cloves, finely chopped

1 medium cauliflower with inner leaves, cut into small florets, stalks and leaves thinly sliced

400g/14 oz can haricot (cannellini) beans, drained

400ml/14 fl oz/1¾ cups whole milk

800ml/28 fl oz/3½ cups vegetable stock

100g/3½ oz/scant ½ cup mature Cheddar cheese, grated

sea salt and black pepper

For the parsley relish

2 large handfuls flat-leaf parsley leaves, finely chopped

1 garlic clove, crushed

finely grated zest and juice of 1 unwaxed lemon

2 tbsp extra virgin olive oil

Melt the butter in a large, heavy-based saucepan over a medium-low heat. Add the onion and celery and cook for 7 minutes until softened but not coloured. Add the garlic and cauliflower florets, stalks and leaves and cook for a further couple of minutes.

Stir in the beans, milk and stock and bring almost to the boil, then reduce the heat slightly and simmer, partially covered with a lid, for 10 minutes until the cauliflower is tender. Stir in the cheese until melted.

Meanwhile, mix together all the ingredients for the parsley relish and season with salt and pepper.

Transfer the soup to a blender (or use a stick blender) and blend until smooth and creamy. Return the soup to the pan and season with salt and pepper. To serve, reheat the soup gently, if needed, then ladle into bowls and top with a spoonful of the relish.

Baked Courgette & Herb Frittata

Saturated Fat 7.4g
Unsaturated Fat 14.6g
Calories 332kcal
per serving for 4

Eggs are wondrous things, super-nutritious and versatile. This recipe is a take on the Middle Eastern dish, *eggah*, which is traditionally flavoured with spices, herbs, vegetables and sometimes meat. This vegetarian version has the distinctive flavour of allspice with lots of dill, coriander, courgette, spring onions and spinach. For convenience, it is baked in the oven and comes with roasted tomatoes.

Serve 4–6
Prep: 20 minutes
Cook: 30 minutes

1 tbsp extra virgin olive oil

6 spring onions (scallions), thinly sliced diagonally

250g/9 oz baby leaf spinach

2 garlic cloves, finely chopped

2 courgettes (zucchini), coarsely grated

6 large eggs, preferably omega-3 enriched

½ tsp ground turmeric

½ tsp dried mint

½ tsp ground allspice

2 handfuls dill, leafy sprigs removed

1 handful coriander (cilantro) leaves, roughly chopped

15g/½ oz butter

300g/10½ oz vine-ripened small tomatoes

55g/2 oz/scant ½ cup feta cheese, crumbled (optional)

3 tbsp toasted almonds, slivered

sea salt and black pepper

Heat a large, ovenproof frying pan (skillet) over a medium heat. Add the oil and spring onions and cook for 1 minute, then add the spinach and cook for 2–3 minutes until wilted, turning the leaves with tongs so they cook evenly. Add the garlic and courgettes to the pan and cook for a further minute, stirring, until softened. Tip into a bowl and leave to cool.

Preheat the oven to 160°C fan/180°C/350°F/gas mark 4.

Mix together the eggs, turmeric, mint and allspice in a large mixing bowl. Add the cooled courgette mixture and half the herbs. Season well with salt and pepper and whisk with a fork until combined.

Add the butter to the frying pan and melt over a medium-low heat. Pour in the egg mixture, then bake for 20–25 minutes until just set and starting to turn golden at the edges. Put the tomatoes on a baking tray (sheet), drizzle over a little oil and roast at the same time as the frittata for 20 minutes.

Leave the frittata to stand for 5 minutes, then turn out onto a plate. Scatter over the remaining herbs, feta, if using, and almonds. Serve cut into wedges with the roasted tomatoes on the side.

Avocado, Broad Bean & Ricotta on Garlic Toasts

Saturated Fat 8.1g
Unsaturated Fat 12.9g
Calories 398kcal
per serving

For anyone who's had their fill of avocados – not me, I hasten to add – this may revive a jaded love of the nutrient-dense fruit. Remember, too, that avocados are one of only two fruits to provide heart-healthy amounts of monounsaturated fat – the other one is olives.

Serves 4
Prep: 15 minutes
Cook: 10 minutes

125g/4½ oz/generous 1 cup frozen broad (fava) beans, defrosted

1 avocado, halved, stoned and flesh scooped out

2 tsp extra virgin olive oil, plus extra for drizzling

finely grated zest and juice of ½ unwaxed lemon

1 tbsp chopped fresh mint, plus extra leaves to serve

250g/9oz/1 cup plus scant 2 tbsp ricotta

15g/½ oz/3 tbsp Pecorino cheese, finely grated, plus shavings to serve

4 large slices sourdough or country-style bread

1 large garlic clove, peeled and halved

sea salt and black pepper

Steam the broad beans for 3 minutes or until tender, then drain, refresh under cold water and pop them out of their grey outer shells to reveal the bright green beans inside.

While the beans are cooking, roughly mash the avocado with the olive oil, lemon juice and mint. Stir in the broad beans and season well with salt and pepper.

Mix the lemon zest into the ricotta with the Pecorino and season.

Heat a griddle (grill) pan over a high heat and chargrill the bread until toasted on both sides. Rub the cut side of the garlic over one side of each slice of toast and drizzle with a little olive oil. Cut each slice of toast in half.

Spoon the ricotta mixture onto the toasts and top with the avocado bean mixture. Drizzle with a little extra olive oil and finish with mint leaves and extra shavings of Pecorino.

Baked Sweet Potato with Black-eyed Beans & Chimichurri

Saturated Fat 3.3g
Unsaturated Fat 16.1g
Calories 457kcal
per serving

My go-to when I'm looking for a simple nutritious meal. Sweet potatoes a great source of fibre. Yet, nutritionally what really lifts them above and beyond regular white potatoes is the presence of the antioxidant beta-carotene, which supports our immune system. Make sure you eat the skin as most of the nutrients are found in or just below it. You could also add a poached egg or crumbled feta for a protein boost.

Serves 4
Prep: 15 minutes
Cook: 1 hour

4 orange (or purple) sweet potatoes, scrubbed
1 tbsp olive oil
2 red (bell) peppers, deseeded and each cut into 8 wedges
400g/14 oz canned black-eyed beans (peas), drained and rinsed
4 tbsp toasted pumpkin seeds
rocket (arugula) leaves, to serve

For the chimichurri dressing

2 handfuls flat-leaf parsley leaves, roughly chopped
1 handful basil leaves, roughly chopped
1 red jalapeño chilli, deseeded and chopped
1 large garlic clove, finely chopped
juice of ½ lemon
4 tbsp extra virgin olive oil
sea salt and black pepper

Preheat the oven to 180°C fan/200°C/400°F/gas mark 6.

Put the sweet potatoes on a large baking tray (sheet) and bake for 1 hour or until tender.

Meanwhile, brush the red peppers with olive oil and place on a separate baking tray. Roast for 30 minutes or until tender and charred in places. Put the peppers in a bowl, cover with a plate, then set aside for 5 minutes – this will make it easier to remove the skins. Peel and roughly chop the peppers and combine with the black-eyed beans. Season with salt and pepper.

To make the chimichurri dressing, put all the ingredients in a mini food processor and pulse briefly; take care as you don't want it to turn to mush. Season, then taste and add more lemon juice if needed.

To serve, slice open the sweet potatoes. Top with the roasted pepper and bean mixture and spoon over the chimichurri dressing. Sprinkle with pumpkin seeds and serve with rocket leaves on the side.

Beetroot, Apple, Walnut & Smoked Mackerel Salad

Saturated Fat 6.4g
Unsaturated Fat 28.6g
Calories 522kcal
per serving

This salad has a distinct autumnal feel, especially with the nutty, earthy flavour of the walnut oil dressing. It comes with a triple dose of good fats thanks to the walnuts, walnut oil and mackerel. The salad is also delicious with a creamy horseradish sauce dressing if you don't have walnut oil – mix creamed horseradish with extra virgin olive oil and loosen with lemon juice, adding a little honey for sweetness, if you like.

Serves 4
Prep: 10 minutes
Cook: 5 minutes

40g/1¾ oz/scant ½ cup walnut halves

2 red-skinned apples, quartered and cored

1 fennel bulb, thinly sliced, fronds reserved

125g/4½ oz mixed leaf salad

4 smoked mackerel fillets, skin removed and broken into large flakes

2 cooked beetroots (beets) in natural juice (not vinegar), weighing about 125g/4½ oz, drained and diced

2 tbsp snipped chives

For the dressing

4 tbsp cold-pressed walnut oil

juice of 1 lemon, plus extra for the apples and fennel

1 tsp Dijon mustard

sea salt and black pepper

Put the walnuts in a large, dry frying pan (skillet) and toast over a medium-low heat for 2 minutes on each side or until starting to colour. Leave to cool, then roughly chop.

Meanwhile, mix together all the ingredients for the dressing. Season with salt and pepper. Taste and adjust the quantity of oil or lemon juice if you need to.

Thinly slice the apples and toss them in a little lemon juice to prevent them discolouring. Toss the sliced fennel in lemon juice for the same reason.

Divide the salad leaves between four plates and top with the apple and fennel. Spoon over half the dressing and toss gently. Top with the mackerel and beetroot and drizzle over a little more of the dressing. Finish with a sprinkling of chives, the reserved fennel fronds and chopped walnuts.

Lamb, Mixed Leaf & Lentil Salad

Saturated Fat 5.1g
Unsaturated Fat 15.7g
Calories 405kcal
per serving

Look for lamb raised on pasture for the highest welfare standards, best flavour and healthiest meat. This dressing is made with hemp oil, which has a lovely nutty flavour that complements the earthy sweetness of the beetroot, lentils and lamb. It is also rich in omega-3 and omega-6 fatty acids, which contribute to good skin, hair and nails. Venison is also good instead of the lamb.

Serves 4
Prep: 15 minutes
Cook: 10 minutes

400g/14 oz grass-fed lamb leg steaks
1 tbsp extra virgin olive oil
4 tbsp non-pareille capers, drained and patted dry
150g/5½ oz mixed leaf salad, including red leaves
200g/7 oz/4 cups cooked green lentils
1 raw beetroot, peeled and shredded
2 tbsp diced red onion
1 tbsp oregano leaves
1 handful flat-leaf parsley

For the hemp dressing
4 tbsp cold-pressed hemp oil
1½ tbsp sherry vinegar
1 tsp Dijon mustard
1 garlic clove, left whole
sea salt and black pepper

Put the lamb in a dish and drizzle over enough olive oil to lightly coat and season with salt and pepper.

Heat a large frying pan (skillet) over a medium-high heat. Add the lamb and cook for 5 minutes, turning once, or until cooked to your liking – it should still be pink in the middle. Remove from the pan and leave to rest on a warm plate, covered, for 5 minutes.

Add the capers to the pan and cook, turning often, for 3 minutes or until they start to turn golden and crisp. Remove with a slotted spoon and drain on kitchen paper.

Mix all the dressing ingredients together and season with salt and pepper to taste.

Place the salad leaves on a large serving plate and top with the lentils, beetroot and onion. Spoon over enough dressing to lightly coat and toss gently. Slice the lamb and place on top of the salad, then top with the herbs. Spoon over more dressing as needed.

Thai-style Omelette with Crab

Saturated Fat 5.4g
Unsaturated Fat 6.4g
Calories 233kcal
per serving

It isn't only oily fish that boasts beneficial omega-3 credentials, crab is also a good source of the fatty acids EPA and DHA, along with the immune-boosting minerals zinc, copper and selenium. It makes the perfect filling for this Bangkok-style street-food dish.

Serves 2
Prep: 10 minutes
Cook: 15 minutes

4 eggs, preferably omega-3 enriched

1 tsp light soy sauce

2 tsp extra virgin coconut oil

100g/3½ oz white crabmeat

2 spring onions, thinly sliced diagonally

1 red chilli, deseeded and thinly sliced

1cm/½ in piece fresh ginger, cut into thin matchsticks

1 handful beansprouts

1 handful coriander (cilantro) leaves, plus extra to serve

juice of ½ lime

freshly ground black pepper

To serve

1 small cucumber, cut into thin ribbons

juice of ½ lime

1 tsp toasted sesame seeds

Beat 2 eggs with ½ teaspoon of the soy sauce in a bowl and season with pepper.

Heat a large frying pan (skillet) over a medium heat and add half the coconut oil.

Pour the egg mixture into the pan, tipping the pan so the egg covers the base evenly. Reduce the heat slightly and cook the omelette for a minute or so, drawing the cooked egg from the sides into the centre to allow the uncooked egg to run to the edge, until the egg is only slightly runny on top.

Spoon half of the crabmeat, spring onions, chilli, ginger, beansprouts and coriander on to the middle of the omelette. Squeeze over a little of the lime juice, then fold in each side to make a square omelette. Cook briefly to warm the filling.

Slip the omelette onto a plate and top with a few coriander leaves and the chilli. Repeat with the remaining eggs, soy sauce and filling ingredients to make a second omelette. Serve with the cucumber ribbons on the side and with a squeeze of lime juice, salt and sprinkling of sesame seeds.

Salmon, Pink Grapefruit & Avocado Salad

Saturated Fat 4g
Unsaturated Fat 18.2g
Calories 427kcal
per serving

This is everything I'm looking for in a salad – it's simple, reviving, vibrant and nutrient-dense with an impressive combination of good fats, protein, complex carbs and fibre. If time is not on your side, use hot-smoked salmon or trout, which is already cooked.

Serves 4
Prep: 15 minutes
Cook: 10 minutes

4 lightly smoked wild salmon fillets

75g/2½ oz/scant ½ cup mixed coloured quinoa, rinsed

1 large pink grapefruit

115g/4 oz rocket (arugula) leaves

1 Little Gem (Boston) lettuce, shredded

½ small red onion, diced

2 tbsp toasted pumpkin seeds

1 handful coriander (cilantro) leaves

For the dressing

3 tbsp hemp seed oil or extra virgin olive oil, plus extra for drizzling

juice of 1 large lime

sea salt and black pepper

Preheat the oven to 180°C fan/200°C/400°F/gas mark 6.

Line a baking tray (sheet) with baking (parchment) paper. Arrange the salmon on the tray, drizzle with a little oil and season with salt and pepper. Cook for 10 minutes or until cooked but slightly pink in the middle.

Meanwhile, cook the quinoa following the packet instructions, then drain and spread out on a large serving plate to cool.

To make the dressing, mix together the hemp seed oil or olive oil and lime juice, then season.

Next, prepare the grapefruit. Slice off the base and stand the fruit on a plate to collect any juices. Working your way around the fruit, cut away the skin and any white pith, then insert the knife between each membrane to remove the segments. Pour any juice left on the plate into the dressing.

When ready to serve, top the quinoa with the rocket, lettuce, grapefruit segments and red onion. Flake the salmon into pieces, discarding the skin, and arrange on top. Spoon over the dressing and finish with the sunflower seeds and coriander leaves.

Chargrilled Sardines with Orange & Olive Salsa

Saturated Fat 3.2g
Unsaturated Fat 8.8g
Calories 259kcal
per serving

Sardines are not only cheap and sustainable, they come with plentiful health benefits. An excellent source of heart-friendly omega-3 fatty acids, vitamins B12 and D and calcium. Look for fish with bright eyes, firm flesh and a shiny skin for optimum freshness and flavour.

Serves 4
Prep: 15 minutes
Cook: 20 minutes

16 sardines, gutted and cleaned
lemon wedges and crusty country-style bread, to serve

For the orange & olive salsa
2 oranges, peeled, segmented and cut into chunks
140g/5 oz black stoned olives, halved
1 shallot, diced
1 tsp extra virgin olive oil, plus extra for the sardines
juice of ½ lemon
2 handfuls flat-leaf parsley, chopped
sea salt and black pepper

Mix all the ingredients for the salsa together in a small serving bowl and set aside.

Rinse the sardines and pat dry with kitchen paper, then brush all over with oil and season with salt and pepper.

Heat a large ridged griddle (grill) pan over a high heat. When the pan is very hot, reduce the heat to medium. Cook the sardines in three batches for 2–3 minutes on each side, depending on their size, until golden with char marks. Serve with the salsa, crusty bread and wedges of lemon for squeezing.

03
Big Plates

Haricot Bean Stew with Nut Aioli

Saturated Fat 1.7g
Unsaturated Fat 8.4g
Calories 238kcal
per serving

Vegetables, olive oil, nuts, pulses and wholegrains are at the heart of the Mediterranean diet and it is this combination of foods, not one food is isolation, that has been found to benefit our health. Recent studies have revealed that a Mediterranean diet causes positive changes in our gut microbiome that have been linked to improved cognitive function, immunity and bone strength.

Serves 4
Prep: 15 minutes
Cook: 30 minutes

3 tbsp extra virgin olive oil

2 onions, chopped

3 garlic cloves, finely chopped

2 bay leaves

400g/14 oz can haricot (cannellini) beans, drained and rinsed

400g/14 oz can chopped tomatoes

2 tsp finely chopped rosemary

1 tbsp fresh oregano or 1½ tsp dried

300ml/10½ fl oz/scant 1½ cups vegetable stock

juice of ½ unwaxed lemon

75g/2½ oz Kalamata olives

3 courgettes (zucchini), quartered lengthways and cut into 1cm/½ in slices

sea salt and black pepper

bulgur wheat, quinoa or wholewheat couscous and Nut Aioli (see page 112), to serve

Heat a large, heavy-based saucepan over a medium heat. Add the oil and the onions and cook, partially covered with a lid, for 8 minutes, stirring occasionally, until softened. Add the garlic and bay leaves and cook for a further minute.

Add the beans, tomatoes, herbs and stock. Stir and bring almost to the boil, then reduce the heat to low and simmer, partially covered, for 10 minutes until reduced slightly. Add the lemon juice and the squeezed lemon skin, olives and courgettes and cook for a further 10 minutes or until the courgettes are just tender. Season with salt and pepper to taste. Serve topped with a good spoonful of the nut aioli and bulgur, quinoa or couscous on the side.

One-pan Piri-piri Aubergine

Saturated Fat 2.6g
Unsaturated Fat 14g
Calories 263kcal
per serving

This meat-free twist on the popular Portuguese piri-piri chicken features plentiful amounts of vegetables, which are roasted and come with a smoky, chilli-hot sauce. The piri-piri sauce is also given a nutritional boost with the addition of roasted red peppers. And the beauty of it all is that it's cooked in one roasting pan. Serve with a rocket salad for a touch of green.

Serves 4
Prep: 20 minutes
Cook: 50 minutes

2 aubergines (eggplants), cut into 2cm/¾ in chunks

2 red (bell) peppers, deseeded and quartered

3 red onions, peeled, halved and each cut into 6 wedges

4 garlic cloves, left whole

6 tbsp extra virgin olive oil

300g/10½ oz small vine-ripened tomatoes

½–1 tsp dried chilli flakes

1 tsp hot smoked paprika

1–2 tsp raw apple cider vinegar

finely grated zest and juice of 1 unwaxed lemon

sea salt and black pepper

To serve (optional)
basil leaves
toasted pine nuts
crumbled goat's cheese

Put the aubergines, red peppers, onions and garlic in a large roasting tin (pan), pour over half the olive oil and toss with your hands until everything is completely coated. Season with salt and pepper and roast for 25–30 minutes until the garlic and red peppers are tender.

Remove the garlic and red peppers from the tin. Put the peppers in a bowl and cover with a plate – this will make them easier to peel. Add the tomatoes to the tin and turn the vegetables, adding a splash of water if it looks dry. Return the tin to the oven for a further 20 minutes until the vegetables are tender and caramelized in places.

Meanwhile, make the piri-piri sauce. Peel the peppers and put them in a blender with the remaining oil, chilli flakes, paprika, vinegar, lemon zest and juice. Squeeze the roasted garlic into the blender, discarding the papery skins, and blend briefly to a coarse purée. Season with salt and pepper, then taste, adding more chilli and/or vinegar if needed.

Serve the roasted vegetables with the piri-piri sauce and topped with the basil, pine nuts and goat's cheese if you like.

Roasted Onions with Nuts & Celeriac Cream

Saturated Fat 14.8g
Unsaturated Fat 22.6g
Calories 654kcal
per serving

Roasting onions in their skins gives them a mild, sweet flavour and they retain much of their goodness. Interestingly, there is some evidence to suggest that the saturated fat in mature cheese is more beneficial to our health than saturated fat from other sources.

Serves 4
Prep: 20 minutes
Cook: 45 minutes

60g/2¼ oz/½ cup hazelnuts, roughly chopped

3 tbsp pumpkin seeds

8 medium onions, loose skin removed and root-ends trimmed

75g/2½ oz/⅔ cup mature Cheddar cheese, grated

2 tbsp extra virgin olive oil, plus extra for cooking onions

100g/3½ oz/scant 2 cups wholewheat breadcrumbs

1 large garlic clove, finely chopped

1 tsp dried thyme

For the celeriac cream

750g/1 lb 10 oz celeriac (celery root), peeled and cut into chunks

squeeze of lemon juice

100ml/3½ fl oz/7 tbsp double (heavy) cream

½ tsp vegetable bouillon powder

sea salt and black pepper

Preheat the oven to 180°C/200°C/400°F/gas mark 6. While the oven is heating, put the hazelnuts and pumpkin seeds on a large baking tray (sheet) and toast in the bottom of the oven for 8 minutes, turning once, or until starting to colour. Remove from the oven and leave to cool, then roughly chop.

Cut a cross, two-thirds of the way down, in the top of each onion and place, cut-side up, in a roasting tin (pan), propping them up with scrunched-up foil if necessary. Pour 2 tablespoons of water into the bottom of the tin and drizzle oil over the onions. Cover with foil and roast for 40 minutes. Remove the foil, open out the onions slightly and scatter the cheese on top. Cook, uncovered, for a further 5 minutes or until tender and the cheese has melted.

Meanwhile, cook the celeriac in boiling salted water for 10 minutes or until tender. (Add a squeeze of lemon juice to stop the celeriac discolouring.) Drain and add the cream and 5 tablespoons of water. Warm through and when it just starts to bubble, stir in the bouillon powder. Tip into a blender and blend until smooth and creamy, then season with salt and pepper. Return the celeriac cream to the pan.

For the crumb topping, heat a frying pan over a medium heat. Add the oil and the breadcrumbs and fry, stirring, for 9 minutes, until golden and crisp. Add the garlic and thyme and cook, stirring, for a further minute. Stir in the chopped nuts and seeds and season. Scatter the mixture over the onions and serve with the celeriac cream

Mediterranean Prawn, Anchovy & Olive One-pan

Saturated Fat 2.3g
Unsaturated Fat 11.3g
Calories 333kcal
per serving

Anchovies do lovely things to a sauce: they 'melt' so their presence is virtually undetectable, yet lend an intense, complex flavour without being too fishy or overpowering. What's more, as an oily fish, they are a good source of omega-3. This seafood dish with added chickpeas and courgettes is perfect served with crusty bread or, for a more substantial meal, you could try wholemeal couscous or bulgur wheat.

Serves 4
Prep: 15 minutes
Cook: 30 minutes

3 tbsp extra virgin olive oil
1 large onion, chopped
1 red jalapeño chilli, finely chopped
4 tsp fresh oregano leaves or 2 tsp dried
2 courgettes (zucchini), quartered and sliced
3 garlic cloves, finely chopped
400g/14 oz can chickpeas, drained
1½ × 400g/14 oz cans chopped tomatoes
4 anchovy fillets in oil, drained and roughly chopped
150g/5½ oz stoned Kalamata olives
3 large basil sprigs
150g/5½ oz baby spinach leaves
300g/10½ frozen, peeled, raw king prawns (jumbo shrimp), defrosted and patted dry
juice of ½ lemon
sea salt and black pepper

Heat a large, deep sauté pan over a medium heat. Add the oil and onion and cook for 7 minutes until softened. Stir in the chilli, oregano, courgettes and garlic and cook for a further 3 minutes, stirring regularly.

Add the chickpeas, tomatoes, anchovies, olives, basil sprigs and 115 ml/3¾ fl oz/scant ½ cup water and bring to a gentle boil. Reduce the heat slightly and simmer, partially covered with a lid, for 15 minutes until slightly reduced and thickened.

Remove the basil, gradually fold in the spinach leaves and keep turning with tongs for about 2 minutes until wilted. Add the prawns and cook for a further 2–3 minutes until cooked through and pink. Season with salt and pepper and finish with the lemon juice.

Golden Cashew Balls in Herb Tomato Sauce

Saturated Fat 10.4g
Unsaturated Fat 28.7g
Calories 626kcal
per serving

Nuts and seeds make a nutritious snack, yet they can be a welcome addition to a main meal. Both the nut balls and sauce can be made in advance and heated through just before serving – they're also delicious with the Cauliflower Cream (see page 112).

Serves 4
Prep: 20 minutes
Cook: 35 minutes

100g/3½/1 cup oz cashew nuts
100g/3½ oz/ ¾ cup mixed seeds
100g/3½ oz/scant 2 cups wholewheat breadcrumbs
1½ tsp dried thyme
2 tsp chia seeds
1 egg, lightly beaten
1 tbsp Worcestershire sauce
1 tbsp English mustard
1 onion, coarsely grated
sea salt and black pepper

For the herb tomato sauce
3 tbsp extra virgin olive oil, plus extra for cooking
3 garlic cloves, finely chopped
2 x 400g/14 oz cans chopped tomatoes
2 bay leaves
1 tbsp tomato purée (tomato paste)
100ml/7 tbsp vegetable stock
2 large sprigs of basil, plus extra to serve
juice ½ lemon
125 g/4½ oz/1 cup mozzarella, drained and torn into pieces

Preheat the oven to 150°C fan/170°C/325°F/gas mark 3. Line 2 baking trays (sheets) with baking (parchment) paper. Put the cashew nuts on one tray and the mixed seeds on the other and toast for 10–15 minutes, turning occasionally, or until they start to colour. Leave to cool, then grind in a mini food processor or blender until finely chopped. Add them to the breadcrumbs and thyme in a large mixing bowl.

Meanwhile, mix the chia seeds into the egg in a bowl and stir in the Worcestershire sauce and mustard. Squeeze out any excess water in the onion, then add to the nut mixture with the egg mixture. Season and stir until combined. Using your hands, form the mixture into 20 walnut-sized balls.

For the tomato sauce, heat a large, deep sauté pan over a medium heat. Add the olive oil and garlic and cook, stirring, for 1 minute. Add the chopped tomatoes, bay leaves, tomato purée, stock and basil and bring up to bubbling point. Reduce the heat to medium-low and simmer, partially covered with a lid, for 20 minutes. Add a good squeeze of lemon juice, stir in half of the mozzarella and season to taste.

Heat a large frying pan over a medium heat and add enough oil to coat the base. Cook the nut balls in 3 batches for 8–10 minutes, turning them occasionally, until golden.

Remove the basil from the tomato sauce. Arrange the nut balls in the sauce, scatter over the rest of the mozzarella, then reheat briefly. Serve topped with extra basil.

Spaghetti with Avocado & Broccoli Sauce

Saturated Fat 4g
Unsaturated Fat 22.1g
Calories 612kcal
per serving

For environmental and sustainable reasons, avocados aren't something we should be eating every day, but there's no denying that they can play a nutritious part of a 'good-fat' diet. Not just good on the ubiquitous toast, avocados also make a deliciously creamy sauce for pasta.

Serves 4
Prep: 15 minutes
Cook: 15 minutes

350g/12 oz wholewheat spaghetti

350g/12 oz broccoli florets, stems sliced and florets halved if large

2 tbsp extra virgin olive oil

2 large garlic cloves, finely chopped

1 large avocado, halved, stoned and flesh scooped out

finely grated zest and juice of 1 large unwaxed lemon

1 small handful mint leaves, plus extra to serve

1 tsp dried chilli flakes

4 tbsp toasted pine nuts

sea salt and black pepper

Cook the pasta in boiling salted water following the packet instructions, then drain, reserving 200ml/7 fl oz/scant 1 cup of the cooking water. Return the drained pasta to the pan.

Meanwhile, steam the broccoli florets and stalks for 4–5 minutes until just tender, then refresh under cold running water until cool.

Put a third of the broccoli florets and all the stalks in a blender with the olive oil, garlic, avocado, lemon zest and juice, mint and 4 tablespoons of water and blend until smooth and creamy.

Add the broccoli mixture to the pasta and pour in enough of the reserved cooking water to make a light sauce. Add the reserved whole florets, season with salt and pepper and warm through gently, adding more water if needed. Serve the pasta topped with extra mint leaves and the chilli flakes and toasted pine nuts.

Japanese Mackerel with Wakame

Saturated Fat 6.9g
Unsaturated Fat 22.1g
Calories 705kcal
per serving

This is such a lovely way to eat mackerel, with the Asian flavours cutting through the richness of the fish. Oily fish, including mackerel, has long been linked to many impressive health benefits, from a reduced risk of heart disease and breast cancer to improved cognitive ability and memory. Make sure you buy the freshest oily fish for the best flavour – a single serving per week is recommended.

Serves 4

Prep: 20 minutes

Cook: 25 minutes

300g/10½ oz/1½ cups brown jasmine rice

20g/¾ oz dried wakame seaweed

3 tbsp tamari

2 tbsp brown rice vinegar

4cm/1½ in piece fresh ginger, peeled and cut into julienne strips

1½ tsp good-quality runny honey

4 large fresh mackerel fillets, halved crossways

4 tsp toasted sesame seeds

8 radishes, thinly sliced

½ cucumber, quartered, deseeded and thinly sliced

1 tbsp olive oil

3 spring onions (scallions), cut into thin strips

½ tsp shichimi togarashi (Japanese 7 spice blend)

sea salt and black pepper

Cook the rice following the packet instructions, then drain and set aside for 5 minutes.

Meanwhile, put the wakame in a bowl and pour over enough cold water to cover, then leave to rehydrate for 5 minutes.

For the marinade, mix the tamari, vinegar, ginger and honey together. Spoon 2 teaspoons of the dressing over the flesh side of the mackerel and marinate until ready to cook – don't leave it for any longer than 20 minutes or the fish will start to 'cook' in the marinade.

Drain the wakame and return it to the bowl with half the sesame seeds, the radishes and cucumber. Pour over half the tamari dressing and mix until everything is combined. Set aside.

Heat a large frying pan (skillet) over a medium heat. Add half the oil and two of the mackerel fillets, skin-side up. Cook for 2 minutes, then turn over and cook for a further 2 minutes or until the skin is crisp and the fish cooked. Remove from the pan onto a warm plate with a slotted spoon and cover to keep the fish warm. Repeat with the remaining oil and mackerel.

To serve, spoon the rice into four large, shallow bowls and top with the wakame salad, then the mackerel. Spoon over the rest of the dressing and finish with the remaining sesame seeds, spring onions and shichimi togarashi.

Coconut Mussels with Noodles

Saturated Fat 16.2g
Unsaturated Fat 5.1g
Calories 555kcal
per serving

Fragrant with lemon grass, lime leaves, ginger and garlic, this noodle bowl features one of our most underrated types of shellfish – mussels. Not only are they sustainable and economical to buy, they come with a long list of health benefits, including heart- and brain-friendly omega-3 fatty acids and energy-boosting zinc, iron, vitamins A and B12.

Serves 4
Prep: 20 minutes, plus standing
Cook: 15 minutes

4 spring onions (scallions), green and white parts separated, thinly sliced diagonally

5cm/2 in piece fresh ginger, peeled and roughly chopped

4 garlic cloves

1 tbsp extra virgin coconut oil

400g/14 oz can coconut milk

3 lemon grass sticks, flattened with the blade of a knife

4 kaffir lime leaves

200g/7 oz medium egg noodles

1kg/2lb 4 oz mussels, cleaned and scrubbed

1½ tsp ground turmeric

1 tbsp light soy sauce

1 medium-hot red chilli, thinly sliced

1 tbsp fish sauce

juice of 1 large lime

sea salt and black pepper

Put the white parts of the spring onions, ginger and garlic in a mini food processor, add a splash of water and blend to a paste. Heat the coconut oil in a large, heavy-based saucepan over a medium heat. Stir in the paste and cook for 1 minute. Add the coconut milk, 200ml/7 fl oz/scant 1 cup water, lemon grass and kaffir lime leaves and bring almost to the boil, then reduce the heat and simmer for 5 minutes, stirring occasionally. Turn off the heat and leave the broth to infuse, covered, for about 30 minutes if time allows.

Meanwhile, cook the noodles in plenty of boiling salted water for 5 minutes or until tender. Drain and refresh under cold running water. Place in a bowl, cover with cold water, then set aside.

Check the mussels and discard any with broken shells or that don't close when tapped.

Remove the lemon grass from the broth and bring the broth almost to the boil over a medium-high heat. Stir in the turmeric, soy sauce, chilli and fish sauce, then add the mussels. Cover with a lid and cook for 4–5 minutes, shaking the pan occasionally, or until the mussels have opened and heated through.

Drain the noodles, pour over just-boiled water from a kettle to reheat them, then divide between four large shallow bowls. Using a slotted spoon, scoop the mussels into the bowls. Taste the broth and add the lime juice and salt and pepper to taste, then ladle it over the mussels. Top with the remaining spring onions.

Herrings in Oatmeal with Yogurt Tartare

Saturated Fat 11.5g
Unsaturated Fat 19.5g
Calories 610kcal
per serving

Herring deserves to feature more in our diet. As well as being cheap to buy and available in sustainable quantities, this oily fish is a great source of omega-3 fatty acids and one of the richest food sources of vitamin D, both of which have been found to protect the heart and support brain function.

Serves 4
Prep: 20 minutes
Cook: 5 minutes

100g/3½ oz/⅔ cup medium oatmeal
2 tbsp milled flaxseeds
8 herring fillets, cleaned, descaled and large central line of bones removed
Dijon mustard, for brushing
25g/1 oz/2 tbsp butter
1½ tbsp extra virgin olive oil

For the yogurt tartare
125g/4 oz/generous ½ cup Greek-style yogurt
2 tbsp chopped flat-leaf parsley
1 tbsp drained and finely chopped capers
2 tbsp drained and finely chopped cornichons
juice of 1 small lemon, plus extra lemon wedges
sea salt and black pepper

To serve
new potatoes in their skins
cooked beetroot, sliced

Mix all the ingredients for the yogurt tartare together with 50ml/2 fl oz water. Season with salt and pepper to taste and chill until ready to serve.

Put the oatmeal and flaxseeds in a shallow dish, season and stir together.

Rinse the herring fillets and pat dry. Lightly brush mustard over both sides of each fillet, then dunk into the oatmeal to coat completely.

Heat a large frying pan (skillet) over a medium heat. Add half the butter and oil and when hot, add 4 of the herring fillets, skin-side up. Cook for 2 minutes, gently pressing the herring flat with a spatula, until golden, then turn over and cook the other sides for 2 minutes or until the herrings are cooked through and the oatmeal is golden. Remove from the pan and drain on kitchen paper while you cook the remaining herring, adding more butter and oil as necessary.

Serve the herring alongside new potatoes, beetroot and the yogurt tartare, with extra lemon wedges for squeezing over.

Roasted Salmon with Soy, Orange & Ginger Dressing

Saturated Fat 3.1g
Unsaturated Fat 10.5g
Calories 301kcal
per serving

There are many good reasons for choosing wild salmon over farmed (see page 29). From a nutritional perspective, wild has been found to be a better balance of omega-3 and omega-6 fatty acids as well as a richer source of iron. Roasting is a simple and quick method to cook the fish, which here comes with an Asian-inspired dressing as well as black rice.

Serves 4
Prep: 20 minutes
Cook: 25 minutes

4 wild salmon fillets
350g/12 oz long-stem broccoli
8 spring onions (scallions), halved lengthways
sea salt and black pepper

For the dressing/marinade
2 tbsp dark soy sauce
1 tbsp toasted sesame oil, plus extra for drizzling
1 tsp good-quality runny honey
finely grated zest and juice of ½ unwaxed orange
2 garlic cloves, crushed
5cm/2 in piece fresh ginger, peeled and cut into thin matchsticks
1 long red chilli, thinly sliced into rounds

To serve
coriander (cilantro) leaves
black rice
lime wedges

Preheat the oven to 180°C fan/200°C/400°F/gas mark 6.

Mix together all the ingredients for the dressing/marinade, adding just half of the chilli. Spoon half of the dressing/marinade over the salmon and leave to marinate until ready to cook, but no longer than 20 minutes or the fish will start to 'cook' in the orange juice.

Meanwhile, steam the broccoli for 2 minutes or until part-cooked, then refresh under cold running water and pat dry with kitchen paper.

Put the broccoli and spring onions on a baking tray (sheet) lined with baking (parchment) paper. Pour over enough sesame oil to lightly coat the vegetables, season with salt and pepper and toss with your hands until everything is coated. Roast for 20 minutes, turning once, until just tender.

Ten minutes before the vegetables are ready, put the salmon and any marinade in a roasting tin and cook in the oven for 10 minutes or until cooked but still slightly pink in the middle.

Serve the salmon with any marinade dressing spooned over the top, sprinkled with the remaining chilli and the coriander leaves. Serve with the roasted vegetables, black rice and wedges of lime for squeezing over.

Greek-style Salmon Fishcakes with Hummus Sauce

Saturated Fat 2.1g
Unsaturated Fat 9.8g
Calories 332kcal
per serving

Salmon retains its impressive omega-3 content when canned. In fact, a US Department of Agriculture (USDA) study found slightly higher levels of omega-3 fatty acids in canned salmon when compared with fresh. The soft bones in canned salmon are also a good source of calcium, so don't throw them away – you won't even know they are there when cooked.

Serves 4
Prep: 25 minutes
Cook: 25 minutes

50g/1½ oz/⅓ cup bulgur wheat
2 x 215g/7½ oz cans wild red salmon
1 tbsp extra virgin olive oil, plus extra for cooking
1 red onion, diced
2 garlic cloves, finely chopped
2 tsp ground coriander
2 tsp ground cumin
½ tsp red pepper flakes or dried chilli, plus extra to serve
1½ tsp dried oregano
½ tsp dried mint
2 tbsp tomato purée (tomato paste)
wholemeal flour, for dusting

For the hummus sauce
400g/14 oz can chickpeas, drained
1 tbsp tahini
juice of 1 large unwaxed lemon and finely grated zest of ½
1 large garlic clove, crushed

wholemeal flatbreads, green salad, lemon wedges, to serve

Put the bulgur wheat in a small saucepan, pour over enough water to just cover and bring to the boil. Reduce the heat slightly and simmer, partially covered with a lid, for 5 minutes or until just tender. Drain the bulgur and tip it into a large shallow bowl to cool.

Remove any skin and large bones from the salmon and flake. Heat a large frying pan over a medium heat. Add the oil and onion and cook for 5 minutes, stirring often, until softened. Add the garlic and cook for 1 minute, then add the spices and herbs. Stir in the tomato purée and cook for a further minute.

Tip the onion mixture into a food processor with the bulgur and half the salmon and pulse briefly until it comes together but is not mushy. Spoon the mixture into a bowl, stir in the rest of the salmon and season. Form the mixture into 8 fishcakes and chill while you make the sauce.

Blend all the ingredients for the sauce with 6 tablespoons of water until smooth and creamy – it should be slightly runnier than regular hummus. Season and set aside.

Just before cooking, lightly dust the fishcakes in flour. Heat a large frying pan over a medium heat. Add enough oil to coat the base of the pan and cook 3–4 fishcakes at a time for 3 minutes on each side until golden and crisp. Drain on kitchen paper and keep warm. Serve with the hummus sauce, warmed flatbreads, salad and with lemon wedges.

Crispy Korean-style Chicken with Gochujang Mayo

Saturated Fat 3g
Unsaturated Fat 7.8g
Calories 302kcal
per serving

This crispy chicken is baked, rather than fried, until crisp and golden and comes with a vibrant red cabbage pickle and gochujang mayo. If you don't want to make the mayo from scratch, simply stir the Korean gochujang spice paste into a good-quality ready-made one.

Serves 4

Prep: 25 minutes, plus marinating
Cook: 35 minutes

2.5cm/1 in piece fresh ginger, finely grated

2 tbsp light soy sauce

2 garlic cloves, finely grated

4 large skinless, boneless chicken thighs

125g/4½ oz day-old seeded wholemeal (whole wheat) bread

1 tbsp milled flaxseeds

1 tbsp black sesame seeds, plus extra for the pickle

wholemeal plain (all-purpose) flour, for dusting

2 eggs, lightly beaten

extra virgin olive oil, for drizzling

Gochujang Mayonnaise (see page 113), to serve

For the pickled red cabbage

1 small red onion, thinly sliced

2 tbsp brown rice vinegar

1 tsp good-quality runny honey

½ tsp dried chilli flakes

175g/6 oz red cabbage, shredded

sea salt and black pepper

Mix together the ginger, soy and garlic in a shallow dish. Place the chicken thighs between 2 sheets of baking paper, then bash with a meat mallet or the end of a rolling pin until flattened evenly, about 1cm/½ in thick. Place the chicken in the soy mixture and spoon the marinade over. Cover and leave to marinate in the fridge for at least 1 hour.

Meanwhile, for the pickle, put the onion in a bowl, pour over just-boiled water and leave for 10 minutes until softened. Mix together the vinegar, honey and chilli flakes in a bowl large enough to hold the pickle. Season with salt. Drain the onion and add to the bowl with the vinegar mixture. Stir in the cabbage and scatter over ½ teaspoon black sesame seeds.

Blitz the bread in a mini food processor, then tip the crumbs onto a plate. Stir in the flaxseeds and black sesame seeds. Put the flour on a separate plate and season with salt and pepper. Beat the eggs in a shallow dish. Preheat the oven to 180°C fan/200°C/400°F/gas mark 6 and line a baking tray with baking paper and drizzle with olive oil.

To coat the chicken, first lightly dust all over in flour, then dunk into the egg and straight into the breadcrumbs. Place on the prepared baking tray.

Drizzle some oil over the chicken and roast for 30–35 minutes, turning once, until golden and cooked through. Serve with the gochujang mayo and pickled cabbage.

Spiced Yogurt-braised Chicken

Saturated Fat 15.2g
Unsaturated Fat 11.6g
Calories 463kcal
per serving

The lightly spiced yogurt curry sauce keeps the chicken beautifully moist and flavoursome during cooking. I prefer to use chicken thighs on the bone in this dish as they add another layer of nutrients to the sauce, including some omega-3 and omega-6 fatty acids, collagen, calcium, iron, zinc and magnesium. The Indian spicing lends itself to a side of brown basmati rice.

Serves 4
Prep: 15 minutes
Cook: 1 hour 10 minutes

20g/¾ oz/1½ tbsp butter or ghee
1 large onion, thinly sliced
4 garlic cloves, thinly sliced
4cm/1½ in piece fresh ginger, cut into matchsticks
1 tbsp coriander seeds, crushed
2 tsp cumin seeds
2 tsp ground turmeric
1 tbsp garam masala
600g/1 lb 6 oz/2¾ cups Greek-style yogurt
8 skinless chicken thighs on the bone
125g/4½ oz baby spinach leaves
squeeze of lemon juice
1 red jalapeño chilli, thinly sliced
1 handful coriander (cilantro) leaves
sea salt and black pepper

Heat a large casserole over a medium heat. Add the butter or ghee and when melted stir in the onion. Cover with a lid and cook, stirring occasionally, for 6 minutes until softened. Reduce the heat slightly, add the garlic, ginger and spices and cook for a further minute.

Stir in the yogurt and 100ml/3½ fl oz/7 tbsp water, then add the chicken thighs. Spoon the sauce over and when it just starts to bubble, reduce the heat to low, cover, and simmer for 1 hour until the chicken is cooked through. Remove the chicken to a warm plate and cover to keep warm.

Add the spinach and lemon juice to the pan and cook, turning the spinach with tongs until wilted, for about 3 minutes. Season with salt and pepper to taste. Serve the sauce topped with the chicken, adding any juices to the plate, and finish with chilli and coriander leaves.

Pan-fried Steak with lots of Beans & Mustard

Saturated Fat 4.8g
Unsaturated Fat 12.9g
Calories 414kcal
per serving

Loosely based on the Italian dish *tagliata*, this warm version of the steak salad features two types of beans and a zingy mustard dressing. Try to buy the best steak you can afford, preferably grass-fed organic meat for ethical and health reasons. Small amounts of good-quality meat, eaten on an occasional basis, provide a range of nutrients, including protein, omega-3 fatty acids, B vitamins, iron and zinc.

Serves 4
Prep: 15 minutes, plus resting
Cook: 30 minutes

2 x 300g/3½ oz grass-fed organic steaks, such as rump or sirloin
4 tbsp extra virgin olive oil
400g/14 oz fine green beans
450g/1 lb small vine-ripened tomatoes, halved
3 garlic cloves, thinly sliced
400g/14 oz can butter (lima) beans, drained and rinsed
1 tbsp wholegrain mustard
juice of 1 lemon, plus extra for squeezing
sea salt and black pepper
Parmesan shavings, to serve

Remove the steaks from the fridge 1 hour before cooking. Season the oil with salt and pepper and drizzle a little over both sides of each steak.

Meanwhile, heat a large griddle (grill) pan over a high heat. Toss the beans in a little of the seasoned oil. Chargrill the beans in four batches for 4 minutes, turning occasionally, until lightly charred in places. Set aside.

Heat a sauté pan over a medium heat. Add 2 tablespoons of olive oil and the tomatoes and cook, stirring, for 5 minutes or until they start to lose their shape. Add the garlic and butter beans and cook for 2 minutes, then stir in the mustard, lemon juice and green beans. Warm through briefly, adding a splash of water if dry, and season to taste. Cover the pan with a lid and set aside.

Reheat the griddle pan and cook the steaks for 2 minutes on each side, depending on their thickness, or until cooked to your liking. Leave to rest on a warm plate, covered, for 5 minutes, then slice diagonally.

Reheat the tomato and beans if liked, then divide between four serving plates and top with the steak. Squeeze over a little more lemon juice and serve topped with the Parmesan shavings.

04
On the Side

Mexican Charred Corn with Lime

Saturated Fat 5.9g
Unsaturated Fat 4.4g
Calories 185kcal
per serving

This is a riff on the popular Mexican street food dish and is a great way to liven up corn on the cob. I've brushed the corn with soured cream, but you could use mayonnaise, double cream or a dairy-free alternative instead.

Serves 4
Prep: 10 minutes
Cook: 15 minutes

4 corn on the cob, husks removed
40g/1½ oz Parmesan, finely grated
4 tbsp soured (sour) cream
1 tsp chipotle chilli powder
lime wedges, to serve
sea salt

Cook the corn in a pan of boiling salted water for 10 minutes or until the kernels are just tender, then drain well.

Put the Parmesan in a wide, shallow dish.

Using tongs, carefully hold a corn over the flame of a hob, turning occasionally, until charred in places. (This could also be done on a barbecue or in a griddle pan.) Repeat until all the cobs are slightly charred.

When ready, brush the still-warm corn with soured cream and sprinkle with the chilli powder. Roll the corn in the Parmesan until coated and eat straightaway with the lime wedges alongside for squeezing over the corn.

Roast Squash with Pumpkin Seed & Miso Dressing

Saturated Fat 1.5g
Unsaturated Fat 6.7g
Calories 192kcal
per serving

Not only does this dressing taste great spooned over the roast squash – or indeed with any roasted vegetable – it comes with numerous health attributes, too. Alongside unsaturated fats, including omega-3, pumpkin seeds provide magnesium, zinc and lignans, which studies have linked with a reduced risk of certain cancers, including stomach. Miso is a fermented soyabean paste and fermented foods have also been shown to improve the health of the gut.

Serves 4
Prep: 10 minutes
Cook: 40 minutes

50g/1¾ oz/5 tbsp plus 2 tsp pumpkin seeds
1 butternut squash
1 tbsp extra virgin olive oil or hemp oil, plus extra for roasting
2 tbsp white miso
2 tsp good-quality runny honey
sea salt and black pepper

Preheat the oven to 180°C fan/200°C/400°F/gas mark 6.

While the oven is heating up, put the pumpkin seeds on a baking tray (sheet) and toast in the bottom of the oven for 7 minutes, turning occasionally, until starting to colour. Leave to cool.

Cut the squash in half lengthways and scrape out the seeds. Wash the seeds to remove any stringy bits, then pat dry. Cut the squash into long wedges and toss in oil until coated. Place in a roasting tin (pan) and roast for 35–40 minutes, turning once, until tender and golden in places.

Meanwhile, toss the squash seeds in a little oil and place on a lined baking tray. Season and toast in the bottom of the oven for 10 minutes or until they start to pop and colour. Leave to cool.

To finish the dressing, put the pumpkin seeds, miso, olive oil, honey and 4 tablespoons of water in a blender and blend until almost smooth. Season with salt and pepper to taste.

Spoon the dressing over the squash and serve with some of the seeds scattered over, if you like, or the seeds can be kept for later and eaten as a nutritious snack. Store in an airtight container and eat within 1 week.

Chargrilled Asparagus with Tahini & Sesame

Saturated Fat 2.4g
Unsaturated Fat 13.1g
Calories 186kcal
per serving

One of my all-time favourite ingredients, tahini is said to contain more protein than milk, is a good source of B vitamins and minerals, including iron, magnesium and calcium, as well as healthy polyunsaturated fats. It makes a creamy sauce for asparagus and is also delicious spooned over leafy greens such as spinach, kale or green cabbage, or even crisp green salad leaves.

Serves 4
Prep: 10 minutes
Cook: 10 minutes

300g/10½ oz asparagus spears, ends trimmed
olive oil, for brushing
2 tsp toasted sesame seeds, for sprinkling

For the tahini & sesame sauce
3 tbsp tahini
1 large garlic clove, crushed
juice of ½ large lemon
2 tbsp toasted sesame oil
sea salt and black pepper

Heat a large griddle (grill) pan over a high heat. Drizzle a little olive oil over the asparagus and turn until lightly coated. Season with salt and pepper. Chargrill the asparagus for 5 minutes, turning occasionally, or until charred in places and just tender. You will probably have to cook it in two batches. Alternatively, steam the asparagus for 3–5 minutes.

Meanwhile, blend all the ingredients for the sauce with 5 tablespoons of warm water in a blender or mini food processor until smooth and creamy. Taste and season with salt and pepper, if needed.

Serve the asparagus with the sauce drizzled over the top and a scattering of sesame seeds.

Roasted Harissa Aubergines with Dukkah

Saturated Fat 1.7g
Unsaturated Fat 8.4g
Calories 94kcal
per serving

A sprinkling of dukkah, the Egyptian spice, nut and seed mix, is a great way of upping the flavour and nutritional value of a dish – think good fats, protein, magnesium, calcium, B vitamins and vitamin E for starters. It pays to keep a jar of dukkah in the fridge ready for sprinkling over salads, stews, soups or grain dishes. For a more substantial meal, serve the aubergines with the Cheesy Polenta on page 108.

Serves 4
Prep: 20 minutes
Cook: 45 minutes

4 smallish aubergines (eggplants)
3 tbsp extra virgin olive oil
2 tbsp harissa paste
1 large garlic clove, crushed
1 handful coriander (cilantro) leaves, roughly chopped
sea salt and black pepper
Greek-style yogurt, to serve

For the dukkah

2 tbsp coriander seeds
1 tbsp cumin seeds
55g/2 oz/½ cup blanched hazelnuts
2 tbsp sesame seeds
2 tbsp pumpkin seeds
¼ tsp dried chilli flakes

Preheat the oven to 180°C fan/200°C/400°F/gas mark 6.

Cut each aubergine in half horizontally through the middle, then make criss-cross cuts over each half. Brush the skin of each aubergine with olive oil and place in a large roasting dish.

Mix the harissa with the garlic, 2 teaspoons of water and rest of the olive oil, then season with salt and pepper. Brush the harissa mixture all over the cut side of each aubergine, making sure it gets into the grooves. Cover the dish with foil and roast for 20 minutes, then remove the foil and roast for a further 20–25 minutes until tender and golden.

Meanwhile, make the dukkah. Toast the coriander and cumin seeds in a large, dry frying pan (skillet) over a medium-low heat for 2 minutes, shaking the pan occasionally. Tip into a bowl and add the hazelnuts to the pan and toast for 5 minutes, turning every so often. Repeat with the seeds, which should take about 3 minutes to toast. Leave everything cool, then tip into a mini food processor and grind to a coarse crumbly mixture. Stir in the chilli flakes and season with salt and pepper. Set aside.

Serve the aubergine, sprinkled with dukkah and coriander, with a spoonful of yogurt on the side. Store any leftover dukkah in an airtight container in the fridge for up to 1 month.

Cheesy Polenta

Saturated Fat 8g
Unsaturated Fat 3.6g
Calories 352kcal
per serving

Butter and cheese bring polenta to life, transforming the ground cornmeal into a rich and indulgent alternative to mash, pasta or rice. Making polenta is a labour of love, yet there is something quite comforting and relaxing about the whole cooking process and, what's more, this gluten-free grain comes with a range of nutrients, including B vitamins, iron, magnesium, zinc and selenium, not forgetting fibre.

Serves 4
Prep: 5 minutes
Cook: 40 minutes

400ml/14 fl oz/1¾ cups whole milk

900ml/31 fl oz/3¾ cups hot vegetable or chicken stock

200g/7 oz/1⅓ cups medium polenta (cornmeal) – not instant/quick cook

50g/1¾ oz Parmesan cheese, finely grated

25g/1 oz/2 tbsp unsalted butter

sea salt and black pepper

Pour the milk and three-quarters of the stock into a medium saucepan and bring to the boil over a medium heat. Reduce the heat slightly and slowly pour in the polenta in a steady stream, stirring continuously with a balloon whisk to prevent lumps forming. Cook for 5 minutes, stirring continuously and swapping the whisk for a wooden spoon when the polenta thickens.

Reduce the heat to low and cook for 30–35 minutes, covered with a lid, stirring every 5 minutes or so, to prevent the polenta sticking to the bottom of the pan. Add more of the stock when needed to make a slightly loose, creamy mixture. The polenta is ready when it starts to come away from the sides of the pan and is thick and creamy, rather than grainy. Stir in the Parmesan and butter and season with salt and pepper. Serve straightaway.

Sun-dried Tomato & Black Olive Tapenade

Saturated Fat 3.2g
Unsaturated Fat 16.3g
Calories 434kcal
per serving

This olive tapenade is given a flavour and colour boost – not to forget heart-friendly antioxidants – thanks to the addition of sun-dried tomatoes. Olives, olive oil and anchovies up the heart-friendly stakes, too. Rich in oleic acid, a type of monounsaturated fat, olives and their oil are thought to help reduce the risk of heart disease as well as inflammation in the body. Anchovies are a good source of omega-3 fatty acids.

Serves 4–6
Prep: 15 minutes
Cook: 5 minutes

175g/6 oz stoned black olives, such as niçoise or Kalamata

6 large sun-dried tomatoes in olive oil, drained, plus 2 tbsp of the oil

2 anchovies in oil, drained

1 large garlic clove, minced

juice of ½ lemon

3 tbsp extra virgin olive oil, plus extra for drizzling

1 large handful flat-leaf parsley leaves, roughly chopped, plus extra to serve

freshly ground black pepper

For the pitta crisps

4 wholemeal (whole wheat) pitta breads

1 tsp hot smoked paprika

Put the olives, sun-dried tomatoes and their oil, anchovies, garlic, lemon juice and olive oil in a mini food processor and blitz briefly until finely chopped. Stir the olive mixture and blitz again, if needed, to a coarse purée. Season with pepper and check the balance of flavours, adding more lemon juice if needed – you shouldn't need any salt. Stir in the parsley and spoon the tapenade into a serving bowl, topping with extra parsley. Set aside while you make the pitta crisps.

Preheat the oven to 150°C fan/170°C/325°F/gas mark 3. Warm the pitta breads – this will make them easier to open out. Cut each bread in half crossways, then run a knife along the inside edge to open it out, then cut down the middle to make two pieces. Return to the oven and cook for a few minutes until crisp. Remove from the oven, drizzle over a little oil and add a sprinkling of smoked paprika. Serve with the tapenade.

Carrots with Walnut Gremolata

Saturated Fat 1.1g
Unsaturated Fat 7.3g
Calories 120kcal
per serving

Gremolata is a classic Italian lemon, herb and garlic condiment that livens up meat and seafood dishes, although it is also delicious sprinkled over vegetables and plant-based dishes. This version has added walnuts for a nutritional boost. Alongside beneficial plant-sourced omega-3, walnuts are said to contain the highest antioxidant levels of any nut.

Serves 4
Prep: 10 minutes
Cook: 30 minutes

40g/1½ oz/generous ¼ cup walnut halves

6 carrots, halved or quartered lengthways depending on size

2 tsp extra virgin olive oil, plus extra for roasting

2 large handfuls flat-leaf parsley leaves, finely chopped

1 large garlic clove, crushed

finely grated zest and juice of 1 unwaxed lemon

sea salt and black pepper

Preheat the oven to 170°C fan/190°C/375°F/gas mark 5.

While the oven is heating up, spread the walnuts out on a baking tray (sheet) and place in the bottom of the oven. Roast for 8–10 minutes, turning once, until lightly toasted. Leave to cool, then roughly chop.

Toss the carrots in a little olive oil in a large roasting tin (pan) and roast for 25–30 minutes until tender.

Meanwhile, make the gremolata. Put the parsley in a bowl with the garlic, lemon zest and juice and 2 teaspoons of olive oil. Season with salt and pepper and mix until combined. Stir in the walnuts just before serving so they keep their crunch. Spoon the gremolata on top of the carrots and serve straightaway.

Cauliflower Cream

I'm a big fan of making simple creamy sauces using vegetables to boost their nutritional value. Cauliflower is used here, but you could easily swap it for leeks, celeriac (celery root) – page 83, broccoli, spinach or peas. This rich, creamy sauce is a great accompaniment to fish, chicken or nut-based dishes.

Serves 4
Prep: 10 minutes
Cook: 5 minutes

1 large cauliflower (leaves removed and saved for another dish), cut into florets
5 tbsp double (heavy) cream or dairy-free alternative
1 tsp vegetable bouillon powder
sea salt and black pepper

Steam the cauliflower for 5 minutes or until tender. Transfer to a beaker with 100ml/ 7 tbsp just-boiled water, the double cream and bouillon powder. Blend using a stick blender until smooth, thick and creamy, adding more water if necessary. Season with salt and pepper to taste – you may not need any extra salt. Serve warm.

Nut Aioli

This dairy-free aioli makes a refreshing alternative to the just-as-delicious Mediterranean olive oil and garlic sauce. Cashew nuts make a surprisingly creamy sauce and come with numerous health benefits, including the ability to reduce high blood pressure and increase levels of 'good' HDL cholesterol. A spoonful of aioli adds the finishing touch to stews, one-pan roasts, grain- and bean-based dishes and more.

Serves 4
Prep: 10 minutes, plus soaking

100g/3½ oz/scant 1 cup cashew nuts
1 garlic clove
juice of ½ lemon
sea salt and black pepper

Put the cashews in a bowl (you can toast them first if you want to give the aioli an extra nutty flavour). Pour over enough cold water to cover and leave to soak for 1 hour.

Drain the cashews and put them in a blender with 4 tablespoons of water and the rest of the ingredients. Blend until smooth creamy, then season with salt and pepper to taste. The aioli will keep for up to 3 days in an airtight container in the fridge.

Homemade Mayonnaise

Look at the ingredients list of shop-bought mayonnaise and you may be surprised to find a whole host of unexpected entries. Yet, homemade mayo is the culmination of a few simple ingredients: egg yolk, oil, vinegar and mustard. Ideally, a mild-tasting oil is best as some oils, such as extra virgin olive oil, can be overpoweringly strong. I've opted for a cold-pressed rapeseed oil (see page 26) but choose a good-quality, non-GM (genetically modified) organic brand. Alternatively, a mild-tasting olive oil is good, too. This mayo can be given an extra oomph of flavour with a little hemp seed, extra virgin olive or walnut oil, but this is optional.

Makes: 200ml/7 fl oz/scant 1 cup
Prep: 10 minutes

1 large egg yolk, preferably omega-3 enriched
large pinch of sea salt
1 tsp Dijon mustard
200ml/7fl oz/scant 1 cup organic cold-pressed rapeseed oil
½ tbsp hemp seed oil, extra virgin olive oil or walnut oil (optional)
1 tbsp raw apple cider vinegar or lemon juice

Using a balloon whisk, mix the egg yolk, salt and mustard in a bowl for about 30 seconds until smooth and creamy.

Gradually, add the rapeseed oil, a drop at a time, whisking continuously until each addition is mixed in. As the mixture thickens – after about half of the oil has been added – you can start to add the oil in a slow, steady stream, still whisking continuously. Take care not to add it too quickly or it can split or curdle.

Once all the rapeseed oil has been added, gradually whisk in the hemp seed oil, or olive oil or walnut oil, if using (it's not necessary to add these if you are happy with a milder-tasting mayo). Then add the vinegar or lemon juice to make a thick, spoon-able mayonnaise. Taste and add extra vinegar or lemon juice and seasoning if needed. The mayonnaise will keep for up to 3 days in the fridge.

Variations:
Garlic mayo: add 1 crushed garlic clove.
Gochujang mayo: add 2 tsp gochujang paste.
Anchovy mayo: add 2 finely chopped anchovies in olive oil.
Chilli mayo: add 1–2 tsp chilli sauce.

05
Sweet Treats & Bakes

Homemade Ricotta with Figs

Saturated Fat 7.8g
Unsaturated Fat 3.6g
Calories 149kcal
per serving

Forget grainy, watery ricotta, this homemade version is deliciously rich and creamy. For the best-tasting ricotta, choose organic whole milk from grass-fed cows. I've served the ricotta with fresh figs, but it would be good with other fruits, roasted or uncooked plums, pears, blackcurrants, blackberries, the list goes on...

Serves 4 with leftovers
Prep: 45 minutes, plus standing
Cook: 40 minutes

900ml/31 fl oz/scant 4 cups whole milk
125ml/4 fl oz/½ cup double (heavy) cream
½ tsp sea salt
3 tbsp lemon juice

To serve
fresh ripe figs, halved or quartered (or a fruit platter with figs, pears, plums, blackberries)
good-quality runny honey
1 handful walnuts, roughly chopped

Heat the milk, cream and salt in a large, heavy-based saucepan, stirring occasionally to prevent it catching on the bottom of the pan, until it reaches 88°C/190°F on a thermometer.

Remove the pan from the heat and stir in the lemon juice, then gently and slowly stir the mixture a few times and leave to stand for 5 minutes. It should start to curdle and separate almost immediately.

Line a sieve with a large piece of muslin, folded into three layers, and place it over a mixing bowl. Pour the milk curds into the middle of the muslin and allow to drip through. Leave to stand for about 2 hours in a cool place or in the fridge if it is a hot day. The ricotta will have the texture of soft cheese when all the liquid has drained through into the bowl. Transfer the ricotta to a bowl and chill until ready to serve. (The drained whey in the bowl can be used as a starter culture for fermented vegetables or added to smoothies or drinks for a protein boost.)

Serve the ricotta with the figs (or your choice of fruit), spooning over some honey and finishing with a scattering of walnuts.

Pan-fried Peaches with Hazelnut Cream

Saturated Fat 4g
Unsaturated Fat 26g
Calories 411kcal
per serving

Nuts make a deliciously rich and creamy alternative to cream made with dairy milk and come with an impressive nutritional profile. Yes, they may be relatively high in fat, but it is the heart-friendly monounsaturated type, and they also provide an abundance of other nutrients, including vitamin E, magnesium and copper, which are believed to help reduce blood pressure and inflammation in the body.

Serves 4
Prep: 10 minutes, plus soaking
Cook: 10 minutes

1 tbsp butter or extra virgin coconut oil

4 large, just-ripe peaches, nectarines or plums, halved, stoned and cut into thick slices

juice of 1 small orange

For the hazelnut cream

180g/6¼ oz/generous 1⅔ cups blanched hazelnuts

250ml/7 fl oz/1 cup plus 2 tbsp hazelnut milk or milk of your choice

1½ tsp vanilla extract

1 tbsp maple syrup

To make the hazelnut cream, toast the hazelnuts in a large, dry frying pan (skillet) over a medium-low heat for 5 minutes, turning them occasionally until they start to colour. (You may need to do this in two batches.) Set aside 30g/1 oz hazelnuts. Put the remaining hazelnuts in a bowl and pour over warm water to cover. Leave to soak for at least 1 hour or overnight if possible.

Drain the hazelnuts and put them in a blender with the rest of the cream ingredients and blend until smooth and creamy. Set aside.

Roughly chop the reserved toasted hazelnuts.

Heat the butter or oil in the frying pan over a medium-low heat, add the peaches and cook for 2 minutes. Add the orange juice, turn the peaches and cook for a further minute. Serve the peaches with any juices from the pan, the hazelnut cream and topped with the chopped hazelnuts.

Baked Stuffed Pears
with Nut Crumble

Saturated Fat 8.1g
Unsaturated Fat 11.1g
Calories 344kcal
per serving

This is crumble with a difference. The nuts add a lovely crunch in contrast to the softness of the pears and cream cheese filling. Since many nutrients are found in or just below the skin of most fruit (and vegetables), the pears are baked skin-on in this pudding but do opt for thin-skinned ones for the best flavour.

Serves 4
Prep: 10 minutes
Cook: 20 minutes

2 large, unwaxed oranges, halved, finely grated zest of $\frac{1}{2}$

2 tsp good-quality runny honey

4 star anise

1 cinnamon stick, broken in half

100g/3½ oz/scant ½ cup full-fat cream cheese or dairy-free alternative

4 slightly under-ripe pears, skin on, with stalks

Greek-style or coconut yogurt, to serve

For the nut crumble

40g/1½ oz/⅓ cup pecans, roughly broken

25g/1oz/⅓ cup flaked (slivered) almonds

2 tbsp unsweetened coconut flakes

Preheat the oven to 170°C fan/190°C/375°F/gas mark 5.

Squeeze the orange juice into a baking dish just large enough to accommodate the pears. Stir in the honey, star anise and cinnamon stick. Mix the orange zest into the cream cheese.

Cut the pears in half lengthways and scoop out the cores using a teaspoon. Place them cut-side up in the baking dish and spoon over the orange juice mixture. Spoon the cream cheese into the dip left by the cores. Bake for 10 minutes.

Meanwhile, mix together the ingredients for the nut crumble. Remove the pears from the oven and spoon over the orange sauce in the bottom of the dish. Spoon the nut mixture on top of the pears and return to the oven for a further 10 minutes or until the pears are tender and the nuts are toasted.

Discard the whole spices and serve the pears with the orange sauce spooned over the top, and a spoonful of yogurt on the side.

Chocolate-coated Nut & Chia Oatcakes

Saturated Fat 3.5g
Unsaturated Fat 4.8g
Calories 154kcal
per serving

Packed with nuts and seeds, these sweet oatcakes have an indulgent dark chocolate topping – although you could leave them plain if you're feeling particularly virtuous.

Makes about 15
Prep: 15 minutes
Cook: 45 minutes

25g/1 oz/about 3 tbsp pumpkin seeds, roughly chopped

40g/1½ oz/generous ¼ cup sunflower seeds, roughly chopped

40g/1½ oz/generous ⅓ cup hazelnuts, roughly chopped

25g/1 oz/generous ⅛ cup chia seeds

90g/3¼ oz/1 cup rolled porridge oats

150ml/5½ fl oz/scant ⅔ cup water

1 tbsp good-quality runny honey

1½ tbsp extra virgin coconut oil

½ tsp sea salt

1 tsp ground cinnamon

2 tbsp milled flaxseeds

150g/5½ oz dark (bittersweet) chocolate, at least 70% cocoa solids, broken into even-sized pieces

Tip the seeds and hazelnuts into a large bowl and stir in the chia seeds and oats. Pour in the water and stir well until combined. Leave for 30 minutes to let the chia expand and for the mixture to become jelly-ish in texture.

Preheat the oven to 160°C fan/180°C/350°F/gas mark 4. Line a large baking tray (sheet) with baking (parchment) paper.

Gently warm the honey and coconut oil in a small saucepan, then pour it over the oat mixture. Stir until well combined, then add the salt, cinnamon and flaxseeds. Spoon the mixture onto the lined baking tray, press it down slightly, then top with a second layer of baking paper. Roll the mixture out to an even layer, about 5mm/¼ in thick. Remove the top layer of baking paper and set aside. Bake for 20 minutes until it starts to turn crisp and golden around the edges. Turn it over by placing the reserved sheet of baking paper on top and, holding both sheets together carefully, flip it over. Remove the top layer of paper. Return to the oven for 20–25 minutes until light golden and crisp – check to make sure it's not burning. Remove from the oven and leave to cool and crisp up.

Melt the chocolate in a heatproof bowl set over a pan of gently simmering water, making sure the bottom of the bowl doesn't touch the water. Once the chocolate has melted, spoon it over the top of the cooled oatcake base, spreading it out with the back of the spoon until it is evenly coated. Leave the chocolate to cool and harden; you could speed this up by placing in the fridge. Break the oatcakes into about 15 pieces and store in an airtight container for up to 5 days.

Almond Pots with Berries

Saturated Fat 6.5g
Unsaturated Fat 26.3g
Calories 486kcal
per serving

Almonds not only come with an abundance of brain- and heart-friendly fats, vitamins and minerals, they also make a surprisingly creamy pudding. Soaking the nuts first helps to make them easier to digest and increases nutrient absorption, and they are much easier to blend. I've used almonds with their skins on as they contain a higher level of antioxidants but opt for blanched almonds if you prefer.

Serves 4
Prep: 15 minutes, plus soaking
Cook: 5 minutes

200g/7 oz/1½ cups almonds
6 soft dried dates, roughly chopped
200g/7 oz/scant 1 cup Greek-style yogurt or dairy-free alternative
150ml/5 fl oz/scant ⅔ cup whole milk or dairy-free alternative
1 tsp vanilla extract
1 tsp ground cinnamon
200g/7 oz berries of choice, such as raspberries, strawberries or blueberries or frozen mixed berries, defrosted

Soak 175g/6 oz of the almonds and the dates in warm water for at least 1 hour or overnight, if possible.

Toast the remaining almonds in a large, dry frying pan (skillet) over a medium-low heat for 5 minutes, turning once, until starting to colour. Leave to cool and roughly chop. Set aside until needed.

Drain the almonds and dates and blend with the yogurt, milk, vanilla and cinnamon until thick, smooth and creamy.

Crush half of the berries with the back of a fork and swirl them into the almond mixture.
Spoon into four small bowls and scatter over the remaining berries and chopped almonds before serving. Chill if not serving the pots immediately.

Seedy Spelt Soda Bread

Saturated Fat 0.8g
Unsaturated Fat 3.2g
Calories 251kcal
per 100g

This bread couldn't be easier to make and uses bicarbonate of soda (baking soda) instead of yeast as a leavening agent. Buttermilk can be found in most large supermarkets, but if you have difficulty finding it, then swap it for plain yogurt mixed with 1 tablespoon of lemon juice. Rich in dietary fibre, this bread comes with a good-fat boost from nutritious seeds.

Makes: 1 loaf
Prep: 15 minutes
Cook: 1 hour

450g/1 lb/2¾ cups wholewheat spelt flour, plus extra for dusting
1 rounded tsp sea salt
1 tsp bicarbonate of soda (baking soda)
2 tbsp pumpkin seeds
2 tbsp sunflower seeds
2 tbsp milled flaxseeds
400ml/14 fl oz/1¾ cups buttermilk

Preheat the oven to 180°C fan/200°C/400°F/gas mark 6. Dust a baking tray (sheet) with flour.

Sift the flour, salt and bicarbonate of soda into a large mixing bowl, adding any flakes of bran left in the sieve. Stir in the pumpkin, sunflower and flaxseeds until everything is combined and make a well in the middle.

Pour the buttermilk into the bowl and gently mix with outstretched fingers to make a soft, slightly sticky dough.

Tip the dough out onto a lightly floured work surface and gently knead it into a smooth ball – try not to over-work it or the bread will be heavy. Place the dough on the floured baking tray and press it down slightly with the palm of your hand.

Cut a deep cross into the top of the dough and sift over a little extra flour. Bake for 50–60 minutes until risen and golden. Tap the underneath of the bread – it is ready when it sounds hollow. Leave the bread to cool on a wire rack.

Mixed Seed & Spelt Crispbreads

Saturated Fat 1g
Unsaturated Fat 4.8g
Calories 121kcal
per serving

Eaten as a snack or served as a base for pâté, cheese or hummus, these seedy crispbreads are loaded with good fats. They have a slightly cheesy flavour thanks to the nutritional yeast flakes, which also adds valuable vitamin B12. It can be difficult for vegetarians and vegans, in particular, to get sufficient quantities of vitamin B12 (found in animal-derived products) in their diet. The nutrient is necessary for healthy nerves, red blood cells and building DNA.

Makes about 15 crispbreads
Prep: 15 minutes
Cook: 1 hour

100g/3½ oz/scant ⅔ cup wholewheat spelt flour

60g/2¼ oz/scant ½ cup pumpkin seeds, roughly chopped

2 tbsp sesame seeds

60g/2¼ oz/scant ½ cup sunflower seeds

2 tbsp chia seeds

2 tbsp nutritional yeast flakes (optional)

2 tbsp milled flaxseeds

1 tsp sea salt

2 tbsp extra virgin olive oil

Mix all the dry ingredients together in a large mixing bowl. Make a well in the middle and pour in the olive oil and 75 ml/5 tbsp water. Mix together with a fork and then your hands to form a slightly sticky ball of dough.

Preheat the oven to 140°C fan/160°C/325°F/gas mark 3. Cut two sheets of baking (parchment) paper the same size as your large baking tray (sheet).

Roll out the dough thinly between the 2 sheets of baking paper – it should be the same size as the paper. Holding both sheets of paper together, carefully lift the crispbread onto the baking tray and remove the top sheet of paper. Bake for 30 minutes until starting to colour around the edges.

Remove the tray from the oven and turn the crispbread over – the easiest way to do this is to place the second sheet of baking paper on top, then carefully and quickly flip it over. Remove the paper on the top and return the crispbread to the oven for a further 30 minutes or until crisp and slightly golden. Lift the paper and crispbread onto a cooling rack and leave to cool and crisp up further. When cool, break into about 15 irregular-sized pieces. The crispbreads will keep in an airtight container for up to a week.

Variation
Herbs and spices such as thyme, rosemary, oregano, caraway seeds, fennel seeds or nigella seeds would also be delicious additions.

Index

Acknowledgements

A great part of this book was created through lockdown, so it feels a real achievement to finish it, let alone for it to reach the bookshelves, and I have to thank a great team of people for their contribution to getting it over the final hurdle. Firstly, my heartfelt thanks to Stephanie Milner and Katie Cowan for their enthusiasm and interest in my idea in the early stages. My gratitude extends to the team at Pavilion – Helen Lewis, for taking up the mantle, designer, Laura Russell, and to Sophie Allen, project editor – it has been such a pleasure to work with you and thank you. Thanks also to editor, Vicky Orchard, and proofreader, Stephanie Evans. The photographers Liz and Max at Haarala Hamilton, you've been stars as usual – thank you so much. And Valerie Berry, well what can I say – fab styling! Last but not least, I have to thank Rachel Vere for prop styling – it couldn't have been an easy job to do during this period of time. Thank you all!